The Neurodivergent Adult's Guide to Professional Exams

Study Systems, Reasonable Adjustments, and Test-Day Strategies for ADHD, Autistic, and Dyslexic Candidates Facing Licensure and Certification Exams

Simon Jack Hughes

This book provides general educational information for adults preparing for professional, trade, and licensure examinations. It is not medical advice, legal advice, or disability advocacy representation. Nothing in this book establishes a clinician and client relationship or an attorney and client relationship. Accommodation and reasonable adjustment policies belong to the testing organizations, professional boards, and regulators that administer each examination, and those policies change. Deadlines, documentation standards, permitted items, and application procedures described in this book reflect publicly available information at the time of writing. Always verify current requirements directly with your testing body before relying on any process described here.

All case studies, worked examples, and named individuals in this book are fictional composites created for educational purposes. Any resemblance to real persons, living or dead, is coincidental. Decisions about medication, including timing and dosage around an examination, belong to you and your prescriber. Do not change any prescribed treatment on the basis of this book. If you are experiencing a mental health crisis, contact your local emergency services or a crisis support line in your region.

The author and publisher make no warranties, express or implied, regarding outcomes from applying the strategies described. The reader assumes full responsibility for the use of the information contained herein.

Published in 2026

ISBN: 979-8-90599-300-8

Table of Contents

Preface

Every profession guards its door with a test. Nursing has boards. Law has the bar. Electrical work, plumbing, counseling, accounting, dispatching, pest control, and dental practice all have their own versions, run by their own boards, with their own rules. The tests differ. The door is the same: on one side is the work you trained for, and on the other side is you, holding a study guide that assumes your brain works in a way it does not.

This book was written for the candidates that exam preparation publishing forgot. If you have ADHD, if you are autistic, if you are dyslexic, or if you carry some combination of these, you have probably already discovered that the standard advice fails you in a specific, repeatable way. The study plan collapses in week two. The accommodation forms read like tax law. The test center lighting takes a third of your working memory before the first question loads. None of this is measured by the exam, and all of it decides the result.

The premise of this book is simple. Your exam problem is an engineering problem, not a character problem. Engineering problems have solutions, and the solutions here come in three layers: a study system designed around inconsistency rather than against it, a practical route through the adjustment and accommodation machinery of the major testing bodies, and a test week protocol that protects the nervous system doing the work.

I have kept the tone practical and the sourcing honest. Where the evidence is strong, I say so. Where the field is still arguing, I show you the argument. Where a testing body's process is unfair, I do not pretend otherwise, and I show you the appeal route.

The credential on the other side of the door is yours to take. This book is about getting the door open.

Introduction

There is a person this book keeps in mind on every page. She is a competent nurse, or he is a competent electrician, or they are a competent therapist. The competence is not in question. Colleagues rely on it. Patients or clients or job sites benefit from it daily. And yet a single standardized examination stands between this person and the license that formalizes what everyone around them already knows.

That gap between demonstrated competence and exam performance is the subject of this book. It is a real gap, it has mechanical causes, and the causes are not laziness, low intelligence, or insufficient wanting.

Professional examinations measure knowledge. They also measure, without ever saying so, a bundle of other capacities: the ability to sustain a study schedule for months, the ability to sit still under fluorescent light for four hours, the ability to decode dense multi-clause questions at speed, the ability to complete registration paperwork across several deadlines, and the ability to regulate a nervous system that knows exactly how much is riding on the next 180 minutes. For most neurotypical candidates, these background capacities are cheap. For ADHD, autistic, and dyslexic candidates, they are expensive, and sometimes they cost more than the knowledge itself.

The exam preparation industry has almost nothing to say about this. Prep courses sell content and schedules that assume steady daily capacity. Study skills books target college students. The accommodation rules that could level the format sit scattered across vendor documents written for evaluators and administrators rather than for you. This book pulls those three missing pieces into one place.

Here is the route. Chapters 1.0 and 2.0 replace self-blame with an accurate mechanical model of how your attention, processing, sensory system, and executive function interact with high stakes testing, and turn that model into a personal exam profile you will use in every later chapter. Chapters 3.0 through 5.0 build the study campaign: architecture first, techniques second, with a dedicated chapter for reading-heavy formats and dyslexic processing. Chapters 6.0 through 8.0 walk the accommodation and reasonable adjustment machinery, from the legal foundations through documentation standards to denials and appeals. Chapters 9.0 and 10.0 cover the days that decide everything: sensory strategy, medication and sleep logistics, and a rehearsed 72 hour protocol. Chapter 11.0 adapts all of it for observed and practical formats such as OSCEs and skills tests. Chapter 12.0 handles results, retakes, and the rejection sensitivity that makes a failed attempt so much more dangerous for this readership than for anyone else.

A note on how to read this book. If you are weeks from a test date, start with Chapter 10.0 and Chapter 9.0, then come back. If an accommodation deadline is approaching, go straight to Chapters 6.0 and 7.0, because those deadlines usually arrive months before the exam and they do not wait for anyone's reading pace. If you have just failed an attempt, Chapter 12.0 was written for this week. The chapters refer to each other by number, so you can enter anywhere and find your way.

One promise before we begin. This book contains no pep talks, and it will not pretend the system is fair. It will show you how the system actually works, what the research actually supports, and how candidates with brains like yours actually pass. That turns out to be enough.

Chapter 1.0: Why Standard Advice Fails

The most reliable predictor of whether a neurodivergent adult passes a professional exam is not intelligence, and it is not how many hours they study. It is whether their study system survives contact with their actual life. The candidates who fail are very often the ones who built the most ambitious plans. The candidates who pass built plans that expected to break. That inversion runs against everything the exam preparation industry teaches, and it is the correct starting point for this entire book, because the industry's advice was engineered for a brain that regulates attention by importance. Yours does not, and no amount of wanting will make it start.

1.1 Two Different Attention Systems

The standard model of studying assumes what might be called importance-based attention. You identify what matters, you allocate attention to it, and attention flows to the assignment. Deadlines help. Consequences help. The bigger the stakes, the easier the focus. Nearly all mainstream study advice is built on this assumption, which is why it leans so heavily on prioritization, scheduling, and reminders of what is at stake.

ADHD attention does not work on that architecture. Decades of research on the disorder converge on a picture of attention regulated by interest, novelty, challenge, and urgency rather than by declared importance (Barkley, 2015; Brown, 2013). The World Federation of ADHD's international consensus statement, which compiled more than two hundred evidence-based conclusions about the condition, is unambiguous that these are neurodevelopmental differences in self-regulation, not motivational failures (Faraone et al., 2021). A licensure exam eight months away is objectively the most important thing in a candidate's professional life and subjectively generates almost no attentional pull at all until the final panicked weeks, when urgency finally arrives and does the job importance never could. Candidates experience this as a moral failing. It is a wiring diagram.

Autistic attention runs on a different but equally non-standard architecture. Murray, Lesser, and Lawson (2005) described **monotropism**, a tendency for attention to flow deeply into a small number of channels at a time rather than shallowly across many. A monotropic study session can be extraordinarily productive, hours of genuine depth on one topic, and extraordinarily hard to redirect. The cost lands at the transitions: switching between subjects, stopping at a planned time, or surfacing from a special interest to review material that holds no pull. Standard advice to study every subject a little each day is close to the worst possible fit for this attention style.

Dyslexic candidates face a third mismatch that has nothing to do with attention allocation and everything to do with the cost per unit of reading. Dyslexia is a persistent difficulty with word-level decoding and fluency that continues into adulthood regardless of intelligence or effort (Snowling et al., 2020). Every practice question, every dense textbook page, every 90 word scenario stem costs a dyslexic reader more time and more working memory than it costs the candidate at the next desk. Multiply that surcharge across a 200 question exam and a six month reading load, and the format itself becomes a tax on the diagnosis.

1.2 The Executive Function Bill

Attention explains why studying does not start. Executive function explains why the surrounding machine breaks. Executive functions are the brain's management layer: working memory, planning, task initiation, time perception, and self-monitoring. Impairment in this layer is central to adult ADHD (Barkley, 2015) and appears, in a different pattern, across autistic adults as well, where meta-analytic work finds broad differences in flexibility and planning (Demetriou et al., 2018).

A professional exam campaign is an executive function stress test wearing a knowledge test's clothing. Consider what the campaign actually demands before a single fact is learned. Register within an eligibility window. Pay fees on time. Book a venue. Track an accommodation deadline that falls months earlier than the exam itself. Build a multi-month schedule. Estimate how long topics will take, a task that collides directly with the distorted time perception documented in ADHD (Barkley, 2015). Initiate studying on days when nothing external forces it. Notice, accurately, whether the studying is working. Each demand is trivial alone. Stacked, they are precisely the load an impaired management layer drops.

This is why so many neurodivergent candidates fail exams they never sat. The knowledge was achievable. The administration was not. Chapter 2.0 will have you map which of these demands your own profile drops most reliably, and Chapters 3.0 and 7.0 are largely machinery for externalizing them.

1.3 Where the Shame Comes From

The following account is a composite, with details changed for anonymity.

Morag had failed her clinical licensure exam twice when she first said out loud that she thought something was wrong with her. Not with her knowledge. She could answer colleagues' case questions on the ward without hesitation, and her supervisor routinely asked her opinion first. What she could not do was make herself open the question bank before 11 p.m., and by then the day had already taken the concentration she needed. Each failed attempt cost a resit fee she did not mention to her family. Before the third attempt she studied harder in the only way she knew, which meant the same system with more hours and more self-punishment attached. She described the weeks before that third sitting as the most disciplined of her life. She scored two points lower than the previous attempt.

Morag's story contains the loop this chapter exists to interrupt. A system mismatched to her attention produced failure. The failure was interpreted as insufficient effort. The interpretation produced more effort inside the same mismatched system, plus a rising load of shame. And shame is not motivationally neutral. Research on procrastination shows that task avoidance operates substantially as short-term mood repair: people delay tasks that have become emotionally aversive, and each delay makes the task more aversive still (Sirois & Pychyl, 2013; Steel, 2007). By the third attempt, Morag's question bank was not study material. It was a shame dispenser, and her brain avoided it with the efficiency of any system avoiding pain.

What finally moved her result was not discipline. It was changing the system: question practice moved to 7 a.m. before the ward took her focus, sessions shrank to a size she could start on a bad day, and a colleague sat with her twice a week doing his own paperwork. The mechanics of why each of those changes works occupy Chapters 3.0 and 4.0. The point here is narrower. Nothing about Morag changed except the engineering.

1.4 The Compensation Trap

There is a predictable objection at this point, and neurodivergent readers usually raise it against themselves: I got through school, so I should be able to get through this. The objection deserves a serious answer, because the answer explains why licensure exams break people who survived everything before them.

Most adults who reach a professional exam with undiagnosed or late-diagnosed neurodivergence got there on compensation. Compensation means effortful workarounds: all-nighters powered by deadline urgency, borrowed notes, charm, last-minute cramming, choosing coursework-heavy paths over exam-heavy ones, and masking, the deliberate performance of neurotypical behavior that autistic adults describe as exhausting and identity-eroding (Hull et al.,

2017; Cage & Troxell-Whitman, 2019). Compensation works, until the load exceeds its capacity. A professional exam raises the load on every axis at once: more material, longer timelines, fewer external structures, higher stakes, and usually a full-time job and adult responsibilities running alongside. Meanwhile the compensation budget is smaller than it was at 20, because masking and effortful self-management have a cumulative cost that autistic adults describe arriving as burnout, a state of exhaustion and reduced functioning distinct from depression (Raymaker et al., 2020).

So the honest reply to the objection is this. You passed school when the load was lighter and the budget was bigger. The strategy did not stop working because you got weaker. It stopped working because it was always the expensive way to do it, and the price finally exceeded the account. The exams did not reveal a deficiency. They revealed a subsidy that had been running, invisibly and at your expense, for 20 years.

1.5 Two Candidates, One Exam

The following are composite cases.

Case A

Lorcan booked his electrical licensing exam nine months out and built the plan the prep book recommended: two hours a night, five nights a week, topics rotating on a printed calendar. For 11 days it held. Then a job ran late, one night was missed, the next night carried a double load that did not happen either, and by the end of week three the calendar had become something he avoided looking at. He did not study again in any organized way until five weeks before the exam, when urgency arrived and he crammed savagely. He failed by six points and concluded he was not a test taker.

Case B

Keva booked the same exam and refused, on the advice of a friend with the same diagnosis, to build anything ambitious. Her plan had one non-negotiable unit: ten questions with the morning coffee she never skipped, answers read aloud to the dog. Most days that was all she did. Some days the ten questions caught interest and became 40. When she missed days, the plan's written rule said the restart cost was ten questions, never a make-up. Across nine months she logged fewer total hours than Lorcan's original calendar promised. She passed with room to spare.

The contrast is not effort, and it is not knowledge. Lorcan's plan was scored by ambition and had a single point of failure: unbroken consistency, the exact resource his profile did not have. Keva's plan was scored by survivability. It anchored to an existing habit rather than to willpower, sized the unit small enough to start on the worst day, and priced re-entry at almost nothing. Retrieval practice, the single most evidence-supported study technique available (Roediger & Karpicke, 2006; Dunlosky et al., 2013), was present in both plans. Only one plan was built so the technique would still be happening in month seven. The evidence on what to practice is settled. The neglected question, and the one this book treats as primary, is what design keeps the practice alive.

1.6 The Core of It

Start here: professional exams measure a bundle of unstated capacities, sustained scheduling, dense decoding, sensory endurance, administrative follow-through, alongside the knowledge they claim to measure, and neurodivergent candidates pay a surcharge on the unstated bundle. Build on that: the surcharge is mechanical. Interest-based attention, monotropic focus, decoding costs, and executive function load are documented properties of these neurotypes, not moral variables, which means more effort inside a mismatched system produces more failure and more shame, not more passing. Then add the third layer: systems can be engineered around fixed properties. Keva did not acquire consistency; she built a plan that did not require it. Morag did not become disciplined; she moved the work to where her attention already was and made starting nearly free.

Everything that follows in this book is an application of that three-step logic to one stage of the exam campaign or another. Chapter 2.0 turns it on you specifically, because "neurodivergent" is a direction, not an address, and the system you build must be fitted to your own profile of attention, sensation, processing, and administration. The fitting requires an honest inventory. That is where we go next.

Chapter 2.0: Mapping Your Exam Profile

The document was one page long. Delyth had printed it herself, four boxes drawn with a ruler, headings written in pen: attention, senses, processing, admin. Under each heading were bullet points in her own handwriting, some crossed out and rewritten. It lived on the fridge for the entire eight months before her accountancy exam, and by the end it was stained with coffee and annotated in three colors. When her study partner asked how she had known to book a separate testing room, she pointed at the second box. When he asked how she had known to stop studying after dinner, she pointed at the first. The page was not a plan. It was a map of the machine the plan would have to run on.

2.1 Why a Profile Comes First

Diagnosis is a category. A profile is an address. Two candidates with identical ADHD diagnoses can have opposite optimal study schedules, because the diagnosis says nothing about when in the day their attention is available, what recruits it, or which administrative tasks their particular executive pattern drops. The diagnostic manuals themselves describe heterogeneous presentations under every label they contain (American Psychiatric Association, 2022), and the practical consequence is that generic ADHD study advice fails almost as often as neurotypical study advice. It is aimed at the category, and you live at an address.

The profile you will build in this chapter is a working document with four sections: attention, sensory, processing, and administrative. Every later chapter in this book asks you to make design decisions, when to schedule sessions, what accommodations to request, which techniques to trial, what to put in the 72 hour protocol, and every one of those decisions is answered by consulting this page rather than by guessing or by copying someone else's system. Candidates skip this step because it feels like a delay before the real studying. It is the opposite. It is the step that stops the next six months of studying from being aimed at someone else's brain.

One boundary before the mapping starts. This is a self-observation exercise, not a diagnostic one. If you suspect an undiagnosed condition, particularly dyslexia or another specific learning difficulty, that suspicion has practical consequences for accommodation eligibility and is worth pursuing formally, a route Chapter 7.0 covers in detail. The profile works either way. It maps function, not labels.

2.2 The Attention Map

The following worked example uses a composite case.

Delyth built her attention map with a two week observation period before she changed anything. The method was deliberately low-effort: a note on her phone, and a one-line entry whenever she noticed herself deeply focused or completely unable to start, with the time of day and what the task was.

Step 1: What the raw log showed

Fourteen days produced 31 entries. Clustered by time, they showed usable focus reliably between 6:30 and 8:00 a.m., a long dead zone from mid-afternoon until roughly 8 p.m., and an unpredictable but sometimes excellent window late at night. Clustered by task, the focused entries were dominated by problem-type work, practice questions and reconciliations, while the failed starts were dominated by reading chapters.

Step 2: What she did with the pattern

The obvious move was to schedule study in the morning window, and she did. The less obvious move mattered more: she stopped assigning reading to any window at all. Reading became something attached to questions, look it up when a question exposes the gap, rather than a scheduled activity in its own right. Her plan now matched not just when her attention arrived but what it arrived for.

Step 3: The complication

The late-night window was her most productive when it appeared, and the temptation was to build the plan around it. She tested that for one week. The window appeared three nights out of seven, and the mornings after those nights were wrecked, taking the reliable 6:30 slot down with them. The decision that followed is the kind a profile exists to force: the late window was treated as a bonus, never a load-bearing part of the plan, because a plan built on an unreliable resource is an unreliable plan. Hyperfocus research supports her caution. The state is real and can be highly productive, but adults with ADHD report limited ability to summon or schedule it (Hupfeld et al., 2019; Ashinoff & Abu-Akel, 2021).

Your own attention map needs the same three ingredients: a time dimension (when focus is reliably available, not when you wish it were), a task dimension (what kinds of work recruit your attention without a fight), and a reliability rating for each window, because Chapter 3.0 will let you build only on the windows you rated reliable.

2.3 The Sensory and Processing Maps

The sensory section of the profile answers one question: what does your nervous system spend working memory on that other candidates get for free? For many autistic and ADHD adults the honest answer is a long list. Overhead lighting with flicker. Keyboard noise from adjacent test stations. The texture of the required lanyard. Background conversation that will not become background. Large surveys of autistic adults find sensory hypersensitivity reported at rates above 90 percent (MacLennan et al., 2022), and the defining feature of the distress, in first-person accounts, is inescapability: input you cannot leave becomes a constant drain on the attention available for anything else.

Map it concretely. List environments that reliably degrade your performance and identify the specific channel: sound, light, touch, smell, movement in peripheral vision, or the social channel of being watched. For each, note whether the problem is the stimulus itself or the inability to escape it. This distinction matters in Chapter 9.0, because testing bodies offer different remedies for each: earplugs from a comfort aid list address a stimulus, while a separate room addresses inescapability, and they are requested through entirely different processes with entirely different evidence requirements.

The processing section maps how information gets in and out. Reading speed against dense text, and whether it collapses further under time pressure. Whether you retain better from hearing, reading, doing, or explaining aloud. Whether negatively worded questions ("which of the following is NOT") cost you disproportionate errors. Whether you lose accuracy or speed first when fatigued. Dyslexic readers should be especially concrete here, because Chapter 5.0 converts this section directly into question-attack routines, and Chapter 7.0 converts it into the functional-impact language that accommodation reviewers require. A useful prompt for this section: on your last timed test of any kind, where did the time actually go? Candidates are frequently wrong about this until they run one timed drill and watch themselves.

2.4 The Administrative Map

The following account is a composite, with details changed for anonymity.

Hemi never mapped his administrative profile, on the reasonable grounds that he already knew he was bad at paperwork. What he had not mapped was the shape of bad. His pattern, visible in retrospect across a decade of adult life, was specific: he initiated administrative tasks promptly when they could be finished in one sitting, and reliably stalled on any task requiring a wait and a return, request a document, wait for it, then submit it elsewhere. His exam campaign hit exactly one task with that shape. It was the accommodation application, which required an assessor's report to be requested, received, and uploaded before a deadline that fell 14 weeks before the exam. He requested the report promptly. It arrived in nine days. It then sat in his inbox, task half-done and therefore invisible, until the deadline had passed by almost a month. He sat the exam unaccommodated, ran out of time with 19 questions unanswered, and failed by a margin smaller than 19 questions.

The administrative map exists to catch exactly this. Its questions: Which of these do you historically drop: starting tasks, finishing tasks, tasks with waits in the middle, tasks with ambiguous next steps, or tasks that require a phone call? What is your track record with deadlines that are far away versus near? Who, if anyone, can hold external copies of your deadlines? Answer from evidence, meaning your actual history with taxes, renewals, applications, and returns, not from intention. The output feeds Chapter 3.0's campaign skeleton, where every administrative task gets a date, and the shapes you drop get externalized to another person or an automated reminder rather than entrusted to the inbox where Hemi's report died.

2.5 Assembling the One Page

The four maps condense onto a single page, and the condensing is not optional. A profile that lives across a notebook is a profile that never gets consulted. The format Delyth used works as well as any: four boxes, each holding only the conclusions, not the observations. Attention: reliable windows, what recruits it, what to never build on. Sensory: top three drains, and for each, stimulus or inescapability. Processing: how information gets in best, where time actually goes under pressure, known error patterns. Admin: task shapes I drop, dates that must live outside my head.

Two rules govern the page afterward. First, it is a living document for exactly the first month, during which real study sessions will falsify some of your self-observations, and then it freezes, because endless profile-tinkering is a respectable-looking form of avoidance. Second, the page is consulted at every design decision in the chapters ahead, and when a technique or schedule fails, the first question is always whether the failure was predicted somewhere on the page. It usually was. The page knew before you did, which is the entire point of writing it down where wanting cannot edit it.

2.6 Putting It to Work

The practical instruction is short. Spend two weeks observing before you optimize anything. Log attention with timestamps rather than trusting memory, because memory about attention is written by the person who wants the late-night window to count. Name the sensory drains and sort each into stimulus versus inescapability. Run one timed drill and watch where the minutes actually go. Pull your administrative history out of old emails and name the task shapes you drop. Then compress all of it onto one page and put the page where the studying will happen.

A senior colleague reviewing your exam campaign would say the same thing in fewer words: stop building until the survey is done. Every expensive failure in the chapters ahead, the collapsed schedule, the missed accommodation deadline, the technique that never fit, is cheaper to prevent here than to repair later. The page costs two weeks of casual noticing. Hemi's blank admin box cost a resit fee, four months, and 19 unanswered questions. That is the trade.

Chapter 3.0: Study Systems That Survive

The field does not have a reliable method for making an ADHD adult stick to a conventional study schedule. That sentence deserves to stand alone, because an entire industry is built on implying otherwise. Planners, apps, accountability programs, and prep-course calendars all sell the same underlying promise, that this time the structure will hold, and the published evidence for durable adherence to self-managed schedules in adult ADHD is thin where it exists at all. The clinical literature is more honest than the productivity literature here: cognitive behavioral programs for adult ADHD spend most of their effort not on scheduling but on shrinking tasks, externalizing structure, and planning for relapse into old patterns (Safren et al., 2005; Solanto, 2011; Ramsay & Rostain, 2015). They assume the schedule will break. So will this chapter.

3.1 The Real Problem Named Precisely

The problem is not starting a study campaign. Almost everyone starts. The problem is the specific failure sequence that follows, and it is worth slowing the film down, because the design solutions in this chapter each target one frame of it.

Frame one: the plan is built in a good week, by an optimistic version of you, and sized to that version. Frame two: a normal-bad day arrives, work runs late, sleep was poor, a child is ill, and the day's block is missed. Frame three: the missed block converts into debt, because the plan's arithmetic says tomorrow now holds two blocks. Frame four: tomorrow's doubled block is aversive enough that it is avoided, and the debt compounds. Frame five: within days the plan itself has become a symbol of failure, and looking at it produces the shame-avoidance loop from section 1.3. Frame six: studying stops entirely until deadline urgency revives it, too late and in panic form.

Notice where the failure actually lives. Not in frame two. Missing a day is a weather event, guaranteed over any multi-month campaign. The failure lives in frames three and four, in a plan whose arithmetic turns weather into debt and debt into avoidance. Conventional advice attacks frame two, trying to prevent the missed day with more commitment. Recovery-by-design attacks frames three and four, and accepts frame two as climate.

3.2 What Does Not Work and Why

The graveyard of failed approaches is worth a short walk, because each headstone teaches a design principle by negation.

The ambitious calendar fails for the reasons frame-by-frame above. Its deeper flaw is that it is scored by coverage, how much material it promises to touch, when the only metric that matters at month seven is whether anything is still happening at all.

Accountability-by-consequence, the study contract with penalties, the app that charges money for missed sessions, fails more interestingly. Punishment arriving after a missed session does nothing to make the next session easier to start, and for a brain already running a shame loop it adds fuel. The procrastination evidence is clear that avoidance is mood repair (Sirois & Pychyl, 2013); adding aversiveness to the task is pouring petrol on the exact fire.

Waiting for motivation fails in the other direction. Interest-based attention means motivation is real and powerful when present, and the error is treating it as schedulable. Section 2.2's rule applies: unreliable resources are bonuses, never foundations.

Marathon catch-up sessions fail on consolidation grounds. A century of research on distributed practice shows that the same hours spaced across days produce dramatically better retention than the same hours massed into a binge (Cepeda et al., 2006). The all-day

Saturday session feels like repayment of the week's debt. Cognitively, most of it evaporates.

What survives from the graveyard is a short list of principles. Score plans by survivability, not coverage. Make starting cheap. Make missing cheap. Never let debt accumulate. Keep the practice distributed, however small the units. The pivot that operationalizes all five is the next section.

3.3 The Minimum Viable Session

The pivot point of this entire chapter is a single design move: define, in writing, the smallest study unit that still counts, and make that unit, not the ambitious block, the load-bearing element of the plan.

A **minimum viable session** is a unit sized to be startable on your worst realistic day. Ten retrieval questions. One flashcard deck cycle. Five minutes of explaining yesterday's topic aloud while the kettle boils. The size is personal, but the tests for it are not. It must be small enough that starting it requires no negotiation with yourself. It must be defined by action, not duration, ten questions, not ten minutes, because clocks invite watching. And it must consist of retrieval rather than reading, because if only one thing is going to reliably happen, it should be the thing with the strongest evidence base behind it (Roediger & Karpicke, 2006; Karpicke & Blunt, 2011).

Around the minimum viable session, three structural rules complete the architecture. First, anchoring: the session attaches to an existing daily fixture, the morning coffee, the commute, the lunch break, rather than to a clock time, because habits recruited from existing routines survive schedule disruption in a way that appointments do not. Second, the flat restart rule: a missed day, or a missed month, is re-entered at the standard unit. No make-ups, no doubled blocks, no debt. The rule must be written into the plan in advance, because the version of you standing in the wreckage of a missed fortnight will not believe re-entry is allowed to be this cheap unless the document says so. Third, the bonus clause: on days when the ten questions catch interest and become 60, the surplus is welcome and is never, under any accounting, banked against tomorrow.

Ambitious blocks still exist in this architecture. They are scheduled into the reliable attention windows from your Chapter 2.0 profile, and they do most of the volume in good weeks. The difference is structural: they are the sail, and the minimum viable session is the keel. Losing the sail slows the boat. Losing the keel is the end of the voyage.

3.4 The Architecture Holding

The following account is a composite, with details changed for anonymity.

Bindi rebuilt her paramedic recertification study around this architecture after two collapsed calendars, and the rebuild's first week nearly convinced her it was a con. Ten questions a day felt insultingly small against a 600 page curriculum, and she said so, out loud, to the friend who had suggested it. What kept her in the system was the written rule she had signed up to: judge it at week eight, not week one.

The log from those eight weeks tells the story better than she does. Weeks one and two: minimum sessions daily, two bonus sessions when the material crossed her actual ambulance shifts. Week three: a run of night shifts, three days missed entirely, and here the architecture earned its keep. The flat restart rule meant day four cost ten questions, the same as any day, and the restart happened. Under her old calendar, she noted, three missed days had been the exact size of hole she never climbed out of. Weeks four through six: the anchor moved from morning coffee to the post-shift bus ride after the coffee slot proved unreliable on nights, an adjustment the plan treated as maintenance, not failure. Week seven contained a genuinely bad stretch, a family crisis, and produced exactly four minimum sessions and nothing else. Week eight: full resumption, no debt, no shame spiral, and a practice-test score 11 points above her baseline.

Two things did not go to plan, and both matter. The bonus sessions she had imagined would be frequent were rare; almost all her volume came from the minimums plus one protected Sunday block. And her original minimum, 20 questions, proved too large to start on night-shift days and had to be cut to ten. The system did not work because it was well designed on day one. It worked because every failure it met was survivable and every adjustment was cheap.

3.5 The Harder Case

The following is a composite case; identifying details have been changed.

Background

Orson, a 41 year old preparing for a welding inspector certification, came to this architecture late, after three failed attempts across four years and with a study-avoidance pattern more entrenched than most. He worked variable contract hours, had unmedicated ADHD diagnosed the previous year, and described the exam materials as producing a physical dread response by the time he rebuilt his approach.

Presentation

The standard architecture stalled immediately. His dread response meant even the ten-question minimum was not being started; the question bank itself had become the conditioned trigger. Anchoring failed too, because contract work gave him no stable daily fixture to anchor to.

Analysis

Two separate problems were tangled: an aversion problem, in which years of shame had made the materials themselves aversive, and a structural problem, in which his schedule genuinely lacked anchors. Treating this as ordinary plan-collapse would have failed. The aversion needed its own ramp before any architecture could function.

Intervention

The minimum was cut to something deliberately absurd: open the question bank, read one question, no obligation to answer it. This is the shrink-the-task logic used clinically in adult ADHD treatment (Ramsay & Rostain, 2015), applied at the extreme end. Anchoring was replaced with event-based triggers tied to his work rhythm, first coffee after any site shift, plus a standing twice-weekly body-doubling session with his brother, who did his own invoicing alongside. Body doubling carried a disproportionate share of his volume, a pattern Chapter 4.0 examines mechanically.

Outcome

Progress was slower than Bindi's and never linear. The one-question minimum took three weeks to grow into a ten-question habit, and one contract change in month four cost him both anchors and required a rebuild. He passed on his fourth attempt with a margin he called embarrassing and his examiner would have called comfortable. He still describes the question bank as something he has a truce with rather than a peace.

Teaching Points

- Entrenched avoidance is an aversion problem before it is a scheduling problem; the ramp back in can start absurdly small and still work.
- Event-based anchors substitute for time-based anchors when schedules are irregular.

- A rebuilt system surviving a mid-campaign rebuild is success, not evidence the system was wrong.

3.6 What Holds Up

Better, but not solved, is the honest summary of this chapter's method. Recovery-by-design does not make studying easy, and it does not make campaigns smooth. Bindi's log still contained missed weeks; Orson's still contained dread. What the architecture changes is the failure mathematics: misses stop compounding, restarts stop requiring heroism, and the campaign is still alive in month seven, which is the entire game. The design principles that earned their place are few enough to hold in one hand. Keel before sail. Actions, not durations. Anchors, not appointments. Flat restarts, written down in advance. Retrieval in the minimum, because whatever happens least must matter most.

What this chapter has deliberately not answered is what to do inside the sessions once they are reliably happening. A surviving system running weak techniques still underperforms, and the technique layer for interest-based, monotropic, and easily bored attention is its own body of evidence and its own set of traps. That layer, body doubling, interest anchoring, novelty rotation, and the honest hierarchy of what actually works, is where Chapter 4.0 begins.

Chapter 4.0: Techniques Built for Your Attention

Zowie's kitchen table held two laptops, one mug going cold, and a spiral notebook that did not belong to her. Across the table her neighbor was answering emails, headphones on, entirely uninvolved in social work licensure. Zowie was 40 questions into a practice block she had failed to start alone on each of the previous four evenings. Nothing about the material had changed. Nothing about the stakes had changed. The only variable that had moved was the presence of another person, working on something else, three feet away, and it had moved the needle from zero questions to 40. She noticed this, wrote it in the margin of her log, and underlined it twice.

4.1 What Happened at That Table

Six months before the kitchen table, Zowie's campaign had looked textbook-doomed. She is a composite, details changed for anonymity, but her log survived and the pattern in it is one this chapter treats as data. Evening study alone: attempted 22 times across two months, completed four times. Weekend library blocks: slightly better on completion, catastrophic on consistency. The prep course's video lectures: watched at double speed while her attention went elsewhere, retaining, by her own testing, almost nothing.

Then three accidental discoveries, none of them from her prep materials. The neighbor arrangement, discovered when a boiler repair put them at the same table one evening. A case-attachment habit, discovered when a practice question about safeguarding thresholds happened to match a live situation from her caseload and became, briefly, the most interesting question she had ever read; she began deliberately pairing question topics with real cases from her working week. And a format rotation, discovered out of boredom: when questions went stale she switched to explaining answers aloud to an empty room in her best case-conference voice, and when that staled she switched to writing gotcha questions designed to trick a hypothetical colleague.

By exam week her log showed the shape of a campaign that had quietly become high-volume without ever containing a single successfully willed solo-discipline session. The question this chapter answers is why those three accidents worked, because each one is a documented mechanism wearing casual clothes, and each can be built deliberately instead of found by luck.

4.2 The Mechanisms Underneath

The kitchen table first. **Body doubling** is the practice of working in the passive presence of another person who is doing their own task. The name comes from the ADHD community rather than the laboratory, and the honest position on evidence is that direct experimental study is thin, while the practice's popularity among ADHD adults is enormous and the mechanisms it plausibly recruits are well documented: social facilitation effects on task performance, externalized accountability, and a reduction in the unstructured aloneness that makes task initiation costly for interest-based attention systems (Barkley, 2015; Steel, 2007). Clinical writing on adult ADHD has folded it into practice as environmental engineering (Ramsay & Rostain, 2015; Prevatt & Levrini, 2015). The evidence reviewed here supports treating it as a first-line tool on cost grounds alone: it is free, it has no failure tax, and when it works it converts unstartable sessions into completed ones.

The caseload pairing is **interest anchoring**, and its mechanism is the least mysterious of the three. If attention in ADHD is recruited by interest and personal relevance rather than importance, then attaching low-pull material to high-pull material is not a trick, it is routing around the known wiring. Depth of processing research adds a second engine: material connected to existing meaningful knowledge is retained better than material processed in isolation, a finding as old as cognitive psychology's modern era. Zowie was not making studying more pleasant. She was making retention cheaper.

The format switching is **novelty rotation**, and it exploits the same wiring from the other side. Novelty recruits ADHD attention; staleness releases it. Rotating formats, questions, teaching aloud, writing distractors, diagram sketching, walking audio review, resets the novelty clock several times per session. There is a bonus hidden in her specific choices: explaining aloud and writing questions are both retrieval and generation activities, which sit at the top of the effectiveness evidence (Roediger & Karpicke, 2006; Dunlosky et al., 2013), while the activity she abandoned, passive video watching, sits at the bottom. Her boredom had, by accident, been steering her up the evidence hierarchy.

4.3 The Honest Hierarchy

A candidate with limited reliable hours needs the effectiveness evidence stated bluntly, because the prep industry sells techniques by engagement, not by retention, and the two rankings disagree.

At the top, by a distance, sits retrieval practice: answering questions, free recall, teaching without notes, anything that forces memory to produce rather than recognize (Roediger & Karpicke, 2006; Karpicke & Blunt, 2011). Alongside it sits distributed practice, already built into Chapter 3.0's architecture (Cepeda et al., 2006). Dunlosky and colleagues' landmark review rated exactly these two techniques as high utility, and rated the student favorites, highlighting, rereading, and summarization as commonly practiced, as low utility (Dunlosky et al., 2013). For this readership the ranking carries an extra edge. Rereading and highlighting are not just weak; they are expensive precisely where you are poorest, consuming reading-heavy, low-novelty hours while producing the feeling of studying without the substance. A dyslexic candidate paying double for every page of rereading is buying the least effective product at the highest personal price.

The practical translation: the minimum viable session is retrieval, always. Reading is demand-led, triggered by what questions expose, as Delyth built it in section 2.2. Video belongs at 1.0 speed with pauses for answer-prediction, or not at all. And the question bank, not the textbook, is the center of the campaign from week one, not a final-month add-on. Candidates resist this because questions feel like testing, and testing feels like judgment before the knowledge is ready. The research position is that the questions are the studying, and the errors are the mechanism, not the verdict.

4.4 Building It Deliberately

The following are composite cases.

Case A

Tovey, preparing for a pharmacy technician certification, engineered all three mechanisms in week one instead of finding them by accident. Body doubling: two fixed sessions weekly, one in-person with a friend, one on a video co-working platform with camera on and microphone off. Interest anchoring: a running list titled "where this shows up at work," one line per study topic. Novelty rotation: a written menu of five formats, with a standing rule to switch the moment a format produced the second consecutive sigh. It held for the whole campaign, with one adaptation: the video sessions worked only when booked with a specific named person, never with an anonymous room. He passed comfortably and kept the co-working sessions afterward for his continuing education hours.

Case B

Rune, facing the same certification, took the same list and hit different weather. The in-person double moved away in month two, and the replacement search stalled for five weeks, exactly the kind of wait-and-return task section 2.4 warns about. Interest anchoring worked brilliantly for clinical topics and failed completely for pharmacy law, which connected to nothing Rune cared about; the eventual workaround was brute novelty, converting the law syllabus into increasingly ridiculous mnemonic drawings. And one rotation format, walking audio review, turned out to be a trap, pleasant, frequent, and untestable, until a practice exam exposed that the walked material had not stuck. Rune passed on the second attempt, six months behind Tovey.

The contrast is deliberate. Same menu, same diagnosis category, different profiles and different luck. Tovey's campaign validates the tools; Rune's validates the maintenance schedule. The tools are not installations, they are subscriptions, and every one of them will need renewal, replacement, or an honest audit somewhere in a multi-month campaign. The audit question that catches most failures early is the one Rune eventually asked about the walking audio: is this format producing retrieval I can verify, or just time I can log?

4.5 Monotropic and AuDHD Adjustments

Everything above tilts toward the ADHD side of the readership, and autistic and AuDHD candidates need the tilt corrected, because monotropic attention changes the calculus in three places.

First, rotation is a cost, not a stimulant. If your attention pays a heavy toll at every transition (Murray et al., 2005), then five format switches per session is a tax schedule, not a technique. The monotropic version runs longer single-format blocks, protects the state once entered, and spends design effort on entry rituals, a consistent physical setup, the same drink, the same opening action, that lower the cost of the one transition that matters, the one into the work.

Second, depth is an asset to harness rather than a distraction to manage. A special-interest-adjacent syllabus area can become the campaign's home base, the territory studied first and deepest, from which the flatter territory is raided in planned expeditions. This inverts the standard advice to allocate time by weakness. Allocating by pull first and weakness second keeps the engine running, and a running engine covering weak areas slowly beats a stalled engine pointed at them directly.

Third, for AuDHD candidates the two systems disagree, and the disagreement is the profile. A need for novelty and a need for sameness can coexist in one campaign by splitting the variables: keep the container identical, same place, same time anchor, same opening ritual, and rotate only the content format inside it. Several of the readers this book is built from report that this single split, sameness outside, novelty inside, was the difference between systems that lasted a week and systems that lasted a season. Your Chapter 2.0 page tells you which variables are which for you. Consult it before installing anything from this chapter.

4.6 Returning to the Start

Go back to the kitchen table. Two laptops, a cold mug, a neighbor answering emails, and 40 questions completed by a candidate who had failed to start for four consecutive evenings. Everything this chapter examined was already present in that scene. The passive presence doing the initiation work that willpower had been failing to do. The retrieval-first format sitting open on the laptop. The margin note, underlined twice, that turned an accident into a system.

Zowie passed, for completeness, though by the time she sat the exam the result had stopped feeling like the interesting part of her story. The interesting part is that her winning techniques were discovered by accident, in month four, after two months of failure that standard advice would have billed to her character. The evidence reviewed in this chapter says none of it needed to be accidental. The mechanisms are documented, the hierarchy is published, and the adjustments for monotropic and combined profiles are mappable in advance from the profile page you built in Chapter 2.0. The table was always available. The neighbor was always next door. What was missing was the frame that said: this counts as studying, and the version of studying you keep failing at does not get to define the term.

Chapter 5.0: Dense Questions and Dyslexic Readers

Somewhere between five and 17 percent of the population shows the persistent word-level reading difficulty that defines dyslexia, depending on where the diagnostic threshold is drawn (Snowling et al., 2020). Take even the conservative end of that range and set it against the format of a modern licensure exam: 180 questions, most of them multi-clause scenario stems of 60 to 120 words, delivered under a clock calibrated to average decoding speed. The arithmetic is stark. On a conservative estimate, one candidate in every 20 sitting a professional exam today is paying a reading surcharge on every single item, in a format where the surcharge compounds 180 times. The exam claims to measure professional knowledge. For this candidate, a meaningful share of the score measures decoding speed instead.

5.1 What the Format Actually Demands

Strip a licensure question to its mechanics and the reading load becomes visible. A typical scenario stem delivers a cast of details, ages, values, times, prior events, in dense prose, then asks a question whose answer depends on perhaps a third of those details. Four options follow, often differing by a single clause. The task is not just reading; it is reading, holding, filtering, and comparing, all inside working memory, all against a clock.

Adult dyslexic readers typically arrive at this task with decoding that is slower and more effortful than their peers', even when accuracy has been substantially remediated over a lifetime (Swanson & Hsieh, 2009; Snowling et al., 2020). Effortful decoding is not just slow. It is expensive, and the currency it spends is working memory, the same limited resource the question's hold-filter-compare structure depends on (Baddeley, 2012). This is why dyslexic candidates so often report a specific failure shape: they understood the question fine, ran out of time, and made careless errors on items they knew, errors that cluster late in the exam as fatigue compounds the cost. Negatively worded stems, the "which of the following is NOT appropriate" construction, are a special tax, demanding an extra inversion operation on top of an already loaded structure.

Two conclusions follow, and they shape the rest of this chapter. First, extended time is not a favor for this profile; it is the removal of a measurement error, which is why it is the standard adjustment for specific learning difficulties across testing bodies, and why the research literature treats the real question as how much time and for whom, not whether (Lovett, 2010; Sireci et al., 2005; Duncan & Purcell, 2020). Chapter 7.0 handles securing it. Second, time alone is not a technique. A candidate with 25 percent extra time and no question-attack routine simply runs the same expensive process for longer. The routine is this chapter's job.

5.2 The Question Attack Routine

The following worked example uses a composite case.

Carwen, preparing for a nursing board exam with formally assessed dyslexia, rebuilt her question process from a timed drill that told an uncomfortable story: averaging 96 seconds per question against a budget of 72, with time lost, on review, almost entirely to rereading stems.

Step 1: Read the actual question first

Her old process read each item top to bottom, the way text arrives. The rebuilt process starts at the final sentence of the stem, the sentence containing the actual ask, then reads the options, and only then reads the scenario. The rationale: knowing the ask converts the scenario from prose to be absorbed into a search target, and searching is cheaper than absorbing. On dense stems this single inversion recovered more time than everything else combined.

Step 2: Mark, don't hold

Everything the working memory was holding moved onto the permitted noteboard: the ask, abbreviated brutally, and the two or three scenario values that bear on it. Externalizing what would otherwise be held is the same principle Chapter 3.0 applied to schedules, applied at 90 second scale. Her error rate on multi-value questions dropped before her speed improved.

Step 3: The inversion flag

Negatively worded stems got a mechanical rule: write "NOT" on the noteboard and convert the task explicitly, cross out the three appropriate options rather than hunt the inappropriate one. The rule costs four seconds and eliminated a category of error she had been attributing to carelessness for years.

Step 4: The triage clock

A per-question budget, posted mentally in thirds: on budget, answer and move; over budget with the answer narrowed to two, mark the noteboard, pick the better candidate, flag for review; over budget and lost, flag and abandon without answering the inner monologue. The complication arrived here, and it is worth staring at. Carwen could not, at first, abandon questions. Leaving an item unresolved violated something deeper than strategy, and her first two drills under the new routine showed her triage rule being ignored under pressure. What worked was rehearsal volume: triage practiced in every drill for six weeks until abandoning a question stopped feeling like an event. The routine is not knowledge. It is a motor skill, and motor skills are built by repetitions, not by agreement.

Her final pre-exam drill averaged 68 seconds per question. The knowledge had not changed in those six weeks. The process had.

5.3 Where the Routine Breaks Down

The routine fails in predictable places, and knowing the failure map is part of owning the tool.

It breaks under fatigue. Late-exam items get the old process, top-to-bottom reading and memory-holding, because trained routines lose to default habits exactly when executive resources run low. The counter is unglamorous: full-length timed practice, not because the knowledge needs it but because the routine has to be rehearsed at the fatigue levels where it will be needed. It breaks on unfamiliar formats, exhibit-based items, drag-and-drop calculations, video stems, which is a scheduling note: obtain the exam's actual format inventory early and build a routine variant per format. And it breaks when it was never really installed, practiced in untimed conditions where its steps are easy, then expected to appear under pressure. The installation standard is simple to state: the routine exists when it runs without being summoned.

One more breakdown deserves its own paragraph because it is invisible from inside. Some candidates using text-to-speech and reader tools throughout their study phase build genuine mastery of material they have never actually decoded under exam conditions, then meet the printed form of their own knowledge for the first time on test day. The tools are legitimate and this book endorses them for the study phase. The rule they require is exposure parity: some regular fraction of practice must happen in the exam's own modality, whatever that will be, including, where a reader or screen-reader accommodation has been approved, practice with that exact delivery, because an unfamiliar accommodation on test day is a new stressor wearing a helpful badge.

5.4 Study Phase Adjustments

The following account is a composite, with details changed for anonymity.

Ledger's dyslexia was assessed at university, and by the time his surveying licensure exam arrived he had a decade of workarounds, nearly all of them built for coursework rather than testing. His study phase adjustments came down to three moves, one of which failed instructively.

The first move was modality shifting: the syllabus's reading load was converted wherever possible into audio, diagrams, and doing. Text-to-speech carried the regulations volumes at 1.4 speed during his commute. Formula-heavy material became worked examples on paper, where his retention had always been strongest. This is standard advice, and it worked as advertised, with the exposure-parity caveat from section 5.3 applied on Sundays.

The second move was aggressive question-bank centrality, for a reason specific to his profile: questions are short-form reading with immediate retrieval attached, the highest ratio of learning to decoding cost available (Roediger & Karpicke, 2006). Long-form rereading, the most expensive activity per unit of retention for any candidate (Dunlosky et al., 2013), is doubly so for a dyslexic one, and his plan banned it outright except as targeted lookup.

The third move failed. Ledger invested heavily in a commercial speed-reading program on the theory that faster reading would shrink the surcharge directly. Eight weeks of drills produced faster page times and, when he tested comprehension honestly, worse retention of dense technical text. The published evidence would have predicted this: reading-speed gains beyond one's decoding capacity trade directly against comprehension, and the trade is steepest exactly where exam text lives (Rayner et al., 2016). The surcharge is real. The routes around it run through format, routine, and time adjustments, not through promises to abolish it.

Ledger passed with a 25 percent time extension, a routine built on Carwen's pattern, and a study phase that had spent his decoding budget like the scarce currency it was. His summary afterward is the chapter's in one line: stop trying to read like them, and start answering like you.

5.5 The Working Knowledge

The practical residue of this chapter fits on an index card, which is where it belongs. Ask first, scenario last. Mark, don't hold. Flag every NOT. Triage on a posted clock, and rehearse the triage until abandoning is boring. Match some practice to the exam's exact modality, including any approved accommodation. Spend decoding currency on questions, never on rereading. And book the timed, full-length drills that install all of it at the fatigue levels where it will be tested, because a routine that exists only when fresh is a routine that will desert you at question 140.

What a working professional should take from the research beneath the card is one sentence of confidence: extended time for this profile is measurement correction, supported across the accommodations literature, and requesting it is not gaming anything (Lovett, 2010; Sireci et al., 2005). What they should take from Carwen and Ledger is one sentence of realism: the adjustment buys back the surcharge only when a trained process spends it well. The next three chapters secure the adjustment. This one built the process that makes it worth securing.

Chapter 6.0: The Adjustment System Explained

On July 26, 1990, on the South Lawn of the White House, George H. W. Bush signed the Americans with Disabilities Act in front of three thousand people, many of them wheelchair users who had spent the previous decades being carried up courthouse steps to demand the right to enter buildings that excluded them. Buried in the statute, far from the headlines about ramps and buses, sat Section 309: any person offering examinations related to licensing or certification for professional or trade purposes must offer them in a place and manner accessible to persons with disabilities, or offer alternative accessible arrangements. Almost nobody sitting a licensure exam today has read Section 309. Every accommodation any of them receives descends from it.

6.1 Before the Statutes

To understand why the current system has the shape it does, start with the problem the statutes were built to fix, because the system's logic, its evidence demands, its definitions, its stubborn insistence on documentation, is all inherited from that founding problem.

Before 1990 in the United States, and before equivalent protections consolidated in Britain, a testing body could simply decline. A dyslexic bar candidate requesting extra time had no enforceable right to it; a blind candidate could be offered nothing; the decision sat wholly with the examiner, and its reasoning, if any, was unreviewable. Rehabilitation Act protections from 1973 covered federally funded entities and left most private testing untouched. What the disability rights movement demanded, and what two decades of activism extracted, was the conversion of accommodation from charity into legal obligation. The ADA in 1990 accomplished that conversion for American testing through Section 309 and its implementing regulations. Britain followed its own path through the Disability Discrimination Act 1995, later absorbed into the Equality Act 2010, which imposes on service providers, including qualification bodies, an anticipatory duty to make **reasonable adjustments** for disabled people (Equality Act 2010).

The conversion came with a price built into its logic. A legal obligation must define who is owed it. Charity can be granted to anyone; a right must be adjudicated. From the moment accommodation became enforceable, the question who qualifies, and on what evidence acquired legal weight, and the documentation machinery that today's candidates experience as bureaucratic hostility began growing from that root. The machinery is not an accident bolted onto the rights. It is the shadow the rights cast.

6.2 What the Law Actually Says

The American framework runs on three load-bearing concepts. A **disability** under the ADA is a physical or mental impairment that substantially limits one or more major life activities, a list that explicitly includes reading, concentrating, thinking, and learning, which is why ADHD, autism, and dyslexia all fall within scope when their functional impact is shown (Americans with Disabilities Act, 1990). The 2008 ADA Amendments Act matters enormously for this readership: it instructed courts and entities to read "substantially limits" broadly, and it barred consideration of mitigating measures, meaning your medication, your workarounds, and your hard-won coping systems cannot be used to argue you out of coverage. The Department of Justice's testing-accommodation guidance adds a third principle with teeth: examinations must be administered so as to measure the candidate's aptitude or achievement, rather than reflecting the impairment, and documentation requests by testing entities must be reasonable and limited (U.S. Department of Justice, 2014).

Considerable weight, the guidance says, should be given to a history of receiving accommodations in similar past settings.

The British framework arrives at similar destinations by different machinery. The Equality Act's definition, an impairment with substantial and long-term adverse effect on normal day-to-day activities, covers the same neurotypes, and the reasonable adjustments duty requires qualification bodies to remove substantial disadvantages that their arrangements create, subject to a limit the framework shares with its American cousin: adjustments cannot alter a competence standard. A regulator may adjust how competence is demonstrated, extra time, a separate room, papers on colored backgrounds, and may not adjust what competence is (Equality Act 2010). That boundary explains most of what candidates find confusing about practical exams, and Chapter 11.0 returns to it.

One structural fact completes the legal map: the law binds the examining entity, but the entity you actually interact with is often a delivery vendor. Pearson VUE and PSI administer hundreds of programs, each with its own owner, and accommodation decisions may sit with the vendor, the program, or the professional board depending on the exam. Knowing which desk holds your decision is the first practical task of Chapter 7.0, because appeals, deadlines, and documentation standards all follow the desk.

6.3 How the Modern Menu Formed

The following account is a composite, with details changed for anonymity.

Mehreen's first encounter with the system, applying for adjustments on a UK accountancy qualification, produced a reaction the history explains: she was startled that a menu existed at all. Extra time in 25 percent increments. A separate room. Supervised rest breaks that stop the clock. A reader, a scribe, screen magnification, colored overlays, papers in specific fonts, permission for earplugs and other comfort items. She had expected to write a pleading letter into a void. Instead there were categories, forms, and precedents, and her assessor knew exactly which phrases the forms wanted.

The menu formed the way case law and administrative practice always form, by accretion. Early adjustments tracked visible physical disability, since ramps-and-readers thinking dominated the ADA's first decade. Specific learning difficulties pushed the menu toward time, and the extended-time literature grew alongside, wrestling with whether extra time advantages everyone or specifically benefits those with disabilities, and settling toward the view that properly targeted extensions primarily benefit the candidates they are meant for (Sireci et al., 2005; Lovett, 2010). ADHD's arrival as an adult diagnosis pushed the menu toward distraction-reduced environments and breaks. Autistic candidates' advocacy is pushing it, unevenly and recently, toward sensory accommodations and clearer communication of procedures. Each addition was fought for by candidates whose needs the previous menu missed, which is worth remembering the next time the forms feel like an obstacle course. The obstacle course is the fossil record of everyone who got through before you.

Mehreen received 25 percent extra time and a smaller room, and her retrospective complaint was not about the outcome. It was that nothing in the process had been discoverable in advance without an assessor who knew the terrain. That gap, between a system that formally exists and a system a candidate can actually see, is the gap this half of the book exists to close.

6.4 The System Meeting Two Candidates

The following are composite cases.

Case A

Barnaby, sitting an American IT certification through a major vendor, approached the system as the law's designers intended. He identified the decision desk before booking, submitted his ADHD documentation through the vendor's portal, received approval for time and a half and a separate room within two weeks, and scheduled with the approval letter's instructions. Total friction: one form, one upload, one wait. His experience is real and common, and this book's warnings should not obscure it: for well-documented candidates on well-run programs, the machinery frequently just works.

Case B

Ephie, sitting a state clinical licensure exam, met the machinery's other face. Her exam involved a board, a vendor, and a separate state agency, and her first application went to the wrong desk, costing six weeks. The right desk wanted documentation newer than her last assessment, which meant a new evaluation at her own expense. The approval, when it came, arrived 11 days before her booked date with instructions to schedule through a different channel, at a center 90 minutes further away, because not every center delivers every accommodation. She sat the exam accommodated and passed, and she describes the process, accurately, as a second unmarked examination in executive function, administered before the real one, to exactly the population least equipped for it.

Both cases are true to the system. Which one you get depends on variables partly outside your control, which program, which state, which vendor, and partly inside it: how early you start, whether you find the right desk first, and whether your documentation meets the standard on first submission. The controllable variables are Chapter 7.0's entire subject.

6.5 What the History Changes

Knowing this history is not decoration. It settles, in advance, the three arguments candidates have with themselves at the application stage.

The first argument is whether asking is legitimate. The history answers plainly: the right was created deliberately, by statute, after decades of organized demand, precisely because informal goodwill had failed. Using a right built for you is not an imposition on the system. It is the system.

The second argument is whether accommodations are an unfair edge. The legal architecture on both sides of the Atlantic embeds the answer in its own limits: adjustments may change how competence is shown and may never change the competence standard itself. A time extension for a dyslexic candidate does not lower the passing bar. It removes a decoding tax the bar was never supposed to include. The measurement literature backs the design where it has been tested (Sireci et al., 2005; Lovett & Lewandowski, 2015).

The third argument is whether the documentation demands mean the system suspects you. It does suspect, in a sense, and the history explains why without excusing the cost: enforceable rights require adjudication, adjudication requires evidence, and the evidence standards calcified during decades when testing bodies fought coverage narrowness in court. The 2008 amendments and current federal guidance pushed back hard toward generosity, and parts of the industry have been slow to notice. You are not paranoid when the process feels adversarial. You are, sometimes, litigating against a fossil.

6.6 Where This Leaves Us

The system you are about to enter is younger than many of the people entering it, built by statute over living memory, and still visibly under construction at its autistic and ADHD edges. It grants real, enforceable rights. It guards them with evidence demands that fall hardest on late-diagnosed adults, on anyone whose childhood records are thin, and on exactly the executive functions the covered conditions impair. Both of those sentences are true at once, and the candidates who do best are the ones who hold both without letting either curdle into cynicism or naivety.

So the question to sit with before turning the page is not whether to engage the machinery. If your profile includes a substantial functional impact on testing, the history says the machinery was built for you, and Chapter 5.0 said what unaccommodated formats cost. The real question is narrower and more useful: what would it take for your application to look like Barnaby's rather than Ephie's, right desk, right evidence, right timeline, first time? That question has a concrete, checklist-shaped answer. It is the next chapter.

Chapter 7.0: Building an Approvable Request

You have the diagnosis, or you are fairly sure you could get it. You have found the testing body's accommodations page, and it links to a form, which links to a documentation guideline, which links to an evaluator guideline, and somewhere in the third document you have stopped reading, because it is written for psychologists and lawyers and you are a candidate with an exam to study for. Every year, capable people close that browser tab and decide it is easier to sit the exam raw. Some of them are reading this chapter after finding out what raw cost. This chapter is the third document, translated, with the reviewer's mind opened up so you can see what your file looks like from the other side of the desk.

7.1 What the Reviewer Is Deciding

Every accommodation review answers three questions, in order, and your file either answers them or it fails. Does this candidate have a covered condition, established by an appropriately qualified professional using recognized methods? Does the condition currently and substantially limit functioning in the activities this exam demands, reading, concentrating, sustaining attention, processing under time pressure? And do the specific accommodations requested logically follow from those specific limitations?

The order matters because candidates habitually over-build the first answer and under-build the second and third. A diagnosis letter, however distinguished its signatory, answers only question one. Reviewers are explicit about this in their own literature: diagnosis alone does not establish functional limitation, and the file's center of gravity must be current impact and its link to the requested adjustment (Gordon & Keiser, 1998; Lovett & Lewandowski, 2015). Vendor guidelines say the same thing in vendor language, requiring documentation that explains the current functional limitation, recommends specific accommodations with specific quantities, and is recent, commonly within roughly three years for conditions whose presentation changes.

Two more facts about the reviewer's frame, both established in Chapter 6.0's legal history, convert directly into drafting strategy. Prior accommodations carry considerable weight under federal guidance, so any history of adjustments, school, university, workplace, other high-stakes exams, belongs in the file prominently, with paper where paper exists. And mitigating measures cannot lawfully count against you in the American framework, so your file can and should describe both the medicated and unmedicated picture, the masked and unmasked picture, without fear that coping well disqualifies you. Late-diagnosed adults, whose whole biography is mitigating measures, need that sentence more than anyone.

7.2 The File, Piece by Piece

The following worked example uses a composite case.

Luan, applying for accommodations on a financial services licensure exam with ADHD diagnosed at 34, built the file that eventually succeeded on the second attempt. The first attempt teaches as much as the second.

Step 1: The failed version

Attempt one contained a one-page letter from the diagnosing psychiatrist confirming ADHD and stating that Luan "would benefit from extra time." It was rejected in nine days: no functional detail, no specific quantity, no testing history. "Would benefit" is the phrase reviewers are trained to discount, since extra time benefits almost anyone. The standard is need, tied to limitation.

Step 2: The evidence inventory

The rebuild began with an inventory, oldest first. School reports at ages nine and 12 describing concentration problems in the exact language of teachers who had never heard of ADHD. A university transcript showing the crash that followed the loss of home structure. An employer email offering a quiet-room arrangement. The diagnostic report itself, which contained functional detail the cover letter had never used. Late-diagnosed candidates always believe they have no childhood evidence; nearly all of them have this kind, descriptions without labels, and reviewers know how to read it.

Step 3: The clinician briefing

Luan's most effective move cost one page. Before the reassessment appointment, she gave her assessor a written brief: the exam's format and duration, the vendor's published documentation guideline, the specific accommodations she believed she needed, and a bullet list of concrete recent examples of impairment under timed, sustained-attention conditions. Assessors are experts in conditions, not in your exam. The brief is not coaching the conclusion. It is aiming the expertise. The resulting report described current limitation against the exam's actual demands and recommended "50 percent additional time and a separate, distraction-reduced testing room" in exactly those words.

Step 4: The submission

The rebuilt file went to the correct desk, identified this time by a fifteen-minute phone call rather than assumption, well before booking, with the prior-accommodation evidence flagged in a one-page cover summary. Approval took 12 days. The complication worth recording: the approval specified scheduling through a special channel with reduced venue choice, and Luan's nearest accommodating center had a five-week wait. Even the successful path costs calendar. Which is the next section.

7.3 The Timeline Nobody Advertises

Work the arithmetic backward from a hypothetical test date and the accommodation timeline reveals itself as the earliest hard deadline in the entire campaign. Scheduling an accommodated seat: often needs two to six weeks more lead than a standard seat. The review itself: publishing bodies quote anything from ten business days to several months, and some board-based exams fix documentation deadlines months before the sitting, bar examiners' deadlines being the notorious example. A new or updated assessment, if your documentation is stale: four to twelve weeks to obtain in most markets, longer where waiting lists are long. Gathering historical records: schools and universities answer in weeks, not days.

Sum the pessimistic column and the answer is stark: the accommodation file should be moving four to six months before the exam, which for most candidates means before serious studying begins. This inverts the intuitive order, in which accommodations feel like a test-week detail. Treat the application as module zero of the campaign. Your Chapter 2.0 administrative map almost certainly flagged wait-and-return tasks as a personal hazard, and this is the highest-stakes wait-and-return task you will ever run, so externalize it accordingly: every date on the campaign wall, every submission confirmed by email you can point to later, and a named second person who knows the deadlines exist.

One cost question belongs here because it changes decisions. A full psychoeducational or diagnostic assessment, privately obtained, runs from several hundred to a few thousand in either dollars or pounds. Whether it is worth it depends on multiplication, not on the sticker: a current, well-built report supports accommodation requests across every exam, workplace request, and further qualification for years. Candidates facing a single low-stakes certification reasonably decide against it. Candidates at the gate of a licensed career are usually buying a multi-use key and pricing it as a single door.

7.4 When the Standard Path Does Not Fit

The following account is a composite, with details changed for anonymity.

Meeka's situation fit no form. Autistic, diagnosed in adulthood, sitting a UK healthcare regulator's competence test, her primary needs were sensory and procedural rather than time-based: a predictable check-in process, a room without flicker, permission for loop earplugs, and written rather than verbal delivery of any procedural changes on the day. The vendor's request categories were built around time, breaks, and readers, and her first conversation with the booking line produced a well-meaning offer of 25 percent extra time, which she did not need, and no mechanism for what she did.

What worked was a shift in strategy from menu-selection to needs-description. Her assessor's letter stopped naming accommodations and started naming functional facts: hypersensitivity to specific auditory and visual stimuli with measurable performance impact, autistic processing differences making unexpected procedural change disproportionately costly, both mapped to the day's known choreography. The letter then invited the test center to propose arrangements meeting those needs, which reframed the center from gatekeeper to problem-solver and engaged the anticipatory duty the Equality Act places on them. The center's eventual offer included a first-slot appointment before the waiting area filled, an agreed check-in script, a seat away from the door, and the earplugs from their permitted list. None of those items had appeared on any form.

Meeka's case carries the section's rule: the published menu is the common case, not the boundary of the duty. Where your needs are non-standard, describe function and impact, invite proposals, get everything agreed in writing, and, the unglamorous coda, bring the written agreement on the day, because the duty is institutional and the staff at the desk at 8 a.m. are meeting you for the first time.

7.5 The Practitioner's Bottom Line

Here is the whole chapter as a senior colleague would give it across a desk. Start the file before you start the flashcards; four to six months out is not early, it is on time. Find the actual decision desk by asking, not assuming. Build the file to answer the reviewer's three questions in the reviewer's order, and put its weight on current functional limitation and the logical line to each specific, quantified request, because that is where thin files die. Harvest your history, school language counts even without labels, and put prior accommodations on page one. Brief your assessor in writing about the exam's demands, since aimed expertise writes approvable reports and unaimed expertise writes diagnosis letters. Describe your functioning without discounting for your coping; the law is on your side there. And where the menu does not fit, describe needs and demand proposals rather than shrinking to fit the form.

None of this guarantees approval, and the next chapter deals with the system's failures honestly. But reviewers themselves, across their own literature, keep saying a version of the same sentence: well-documented requests with coherent functional evidence are mostly granted, and the files that fail are mostly files that never made the case (Gordon & Keiser, 1998; Lovett & Lewandowski, 2015). Making the case is a buildable, finite task. You now have the build order.

Chapter 8.0: Denials, Appeals, and Rights

The legal framework gives considerable weight to a history of prior accommodations, and testing bodies have denied candidates who documented twenty years of them. Federal guidance instructs that documentation demands be reasonable and limited, and candidates have paid thousands for seven-hour evaluations only to be told the evidence remains insufficient. Both halves of each sentence are true, currently, simultaneously. This chapter is about the gap between them: why well-founded requests still get denied, what the honest disagreement inside the review system looks like, and what a denied candidate can actually do, from internal appeal to federal complaint to the pragmatic decision to sit anyway.

8.1 The Disagreement Stated Fairly

Behind every contested denial sits a genuine dispute about evidence standards, and pretending it is simple bad faith on either side will get you nowhere useful. It is worth stating both positions at strength, because your appeal will be read by someone holding one of them.

The strict position, held by many reviewing consultants and visible throughout bar examiner literature, runs like this. Accommodations exist to correct measurement error for genuinely limited candidates, and high-stakes gateways attract requests from candidates whose evidence amounts to self-report plus a supportive clinician. Self-reported symptoms may support a clinical diagnosis, the strict reviewers argue, but diagnosis is not limitation, and someone who progressed through school and university without accommodations, earning ordinary grades, has demonstrated average functioning under standard conditions; granting extra time in such cases advantages one candidate over others and erodes the meaning of the adjustment (National Conference of Bar Examiners, 2016). On this view, demanding objective, historical, multi-source evidence is not hostility. It is what taking the accommodation seriously looks like.

The generous position, held by disability advocates, much of the clinical field, and increasingly by legislatures and courts, answers each point. The average-grades argument ignores compensation cost: late-diagnosed adults achieve ordinary results at extraordinary private expense, and the law explicitly forbids counting mitigating measures against coverage, a bar the average-grades logic walks straight through. The childhood-records demand falls hardest on exactly the populations the diagnostic system historically missed, including women and anyone assessed in eras or places where the labels did not reach. The costs are not symmetric: a wrongly granted extension mildly advantages one candidate, while a wrongly denied one can end a career the person is competent to practice. And functional limitation in real testing conditions is precisely what a supportive clinician who has actually examined the candidate is qualified to attest, so discounting clinical judgment in favor of decades-old paper inverts the reliability of the evidence.

8.2 What the Record Shows

Neither side wins this argument in the abstract, but the recent record shows which way the institutional weather is moving, and a denied candidate should know the direction.

Courts have begun overturning board denials on exactly the generous position's logic. In late 2023, Maryland's highest court reversed its own bar examiners' refusal of 50 percent additional time for a candidate with ADHD, holding that his documented disability and history of law school accommodations met the ADA's standard and that the requested adjustment was reasonable and consistent with the exam's purpose (In the Matter of Chavis, 2023). The federal testing-accommodation guidance already pointed the same way, instructing entities to give considerable weight to past accommodations and warning against burdensome documentation demands (U.S. Department of Justice, 2014). State legislatures have started intervening directly, with bills requiring testing entities to honor accommodations previously granted on other high-stakes examinations, and some licensing bodies have adopted that reciprocity voluntarily: California's bar, for instance, streamlines approval for candidates with prior accommodations on a listed set of major standardized tests.

Set against that weather, the strict position still controls many desks day to day, and the practical reading for a candidate is double-edged. Your first submission should be built for the strict reviewer, evidence-dense, history-forward, functionally specific, because building for the generous one and hoping is how first denials happen. Your appeal, if it comes to that, should be built on the generous framework's now-considerable institutional backing, because that is the direction reversals run.

8.3 Reading and Answering a Denial

The following is a composite case; identifying details have been changed.

Background

Cashel, a 38 year old candidate for a state counseling licensure exam, received a denial eight weeks before his test date. His file had contained a two-year-old diagnostic report for ADHD, a supporting letter from his current therapist, and a personal statement. The denial letter cited insufficient evidence of current functional limitation and noted the absence of any record of prior accommodations.

Presentation

His first response was the one this book's readership will recognize: a rejection-sensitivity spiral lasting most of a week, in which the letter was reread as a verdict on his legitimacy rather than on his paperwork, followed by an impulse to withdraw the request entirely and sit unaccommodated rather than face a second refusal.

Analysis

Read technically, the denial was a specification, not a verdict. Insufficient evidence of current limitation identified a missing document class: standardized functional evidence newer than the diagnostic report. The prior-accommodations observation identified a gap his history genuinely contained, which meant his appeal needed to explain the gap, late diagnosis, rather than fill it. Denial letters are written in a genre, and the genre's convention is to name what would change the outcome. Most candidates read them for the no and miss the shopping list.

Intervention

The appeal package took five weeks of the eight. His assessor produced an updated report responding point-by-point to the denial's language, including timed-task performance data and explicit linkage of each limitation to the exam's format. The gap explanation entered through a one-page chronology: assessment at 36, with the school-report language from ages eight through 16 quoted verbatim to show the impairment predated the label. A cover letter cited the federal guidance's mitigating-measures and past-accommodations principles by name. He also, on advice, requested a deadline extension for his test date pending the appeal, which the board granted routinely and which he had assumed was impossible.

Outcome

The appeal succeeded in part: 25 percent additional time and a separate room, against the 50 percent requested. He took the partial grant and passed with 11 minutes to spare, which he noted was less margin than the denied second 25 percent would have provided. The system's last word was neither vindication nor injustice but something more ordinary: a negotiated settlement he had nearly abandoned at the first no.

Teaching Points

- A denial letter is a specification document; extract the missing evidence class before appealing.
- Gaps in accommodation history are explained, not apologized for, and late diagnosis is an explanation with legal standing.
- Ask about deadline extensions pending appeal; the assumption that dates are immovable kills more appeals than reviewers do.

8.4 The Escalation Ladder

When internal appeal fails, the ladder continues, and each rung has a realistic cost profile a candidate should see before climbing.

Rung one is the vendor or board's own second-level review, where one exists; some programs route appeals to an external consultant, and the reversal rate, while unpublished, is not negligible for evidence-supplemented appeals. Rung two, in the United States, is a complaint to the Department of Justice under the ADA's testing provisions, free to file, potentially slow, and most powerful where the denial pattern is systemic; DOJ settlement agreements with testing entities have repeatedly reshaped industry documentation practice. Rung two in Britain runs through the qualification body's complaints process toward the Equality and Human Rights Commission's enforcement remit or a county court discrimination claim. Rung three is private litigation, which the Chavis reversal shows can succeed, and which costs money, months, and attention, three currencies an exam candidate is already spending elsewhere.

The honest strategic note about the ladder is about time. Rungs two and three usually resolve after your test date. Their realistic function for an individual candidate is to fix the next attempt, or the next candidate, not the booked sitting, and factoring that into the decision is not defeatism, it is scheduling.

8.5 Sitting Anyway

The following account is a composite, with details changed for anonymity.

Scotia ran out of ladder. Her appeal on a dispatcher certification exam was refused a second time, 19 days before a test date that her employment offer would not survive moving, and the choice in front of her was the one this section exists for: withdraw, or sit unaccommodated. She sat. What made the sitting survivable was treating the denial as a design input rather than only an injury. The 19 days were rebuilt around the specific limitation the accommodation would have addressed: her triage routine from timed drills was retrained at full exam length, twice, at the fatigue levels where it mattered; her section pacing was recalculated for the standard clock with abandonment thresholds she wrote on the noteboard in the first minute; and the sensory plan from her earlier application, first slot of the morning, earplugs from the permitted list, seat away from the door, turned out to be substantially deliverable through ordinary booking choices and polite requests that required no approval at all.

She passed by a margin she describes as two questions and a good night's sleep. The point of her story is emphatically not that accommodations are optional; Chapter 5.0's arithmetic stands, and she carried a measurable, unjust surcharge into that room. The point is narrower. A denial takes the adjustment. It does not take the profile knowledge, the routines, the informal arrangements, or the campaign, and a candidate forced onto the standard clock still controls more variables than the denial letter implies.

8.6 The Honest Summary

Settled, first. The legal right exists, ADHD, autism, and dyslexia are within its scope, mitigating measures cannot lawfully be held against you, past accommodations carry recognized weight, and courts have shown they will reverse boards that ignore all this. Well-built files are mostly approved, and denial letters mostly specify their own remedy. Contested, second, and honestly so. Evidence standards for late-diagnosed adults remain a live disagreement inside the review system; the strict position still staffs many desks; documentation costs fall on the candidate in money and executive function; and the escalation machinery mostly runs slower than any single test date. Where that leaves you is neither reassured nor resigned but equipped: build the first file for the strict reviewer, read any denial as a specification, appeal on the generous framework's growing institutional weight, ask for the deadline extension, and if you must sit anyway, sit as Scotia did, with the campaign the denial could not touch. The field's argument about evidence standards will not be settled by your exam date. Your file does not need it to be.

Chapter 9.0: Sensory Strategy for Test Day

Revel and Kylara sat the same insurance licensing exam, in the same test center, four days apart. Both autistic, both well prepared, both scoring within two points of each other on their final practice tests. Revel finished with 20 minutes to spare and passed comfortably. Kylara left question 71 of 150 unanswered when time expired and failed by nine points. The knowledge gap between them was, by every measurable indicator, close to zero. What differed was that Revel had spent 90 minutes, three weeks earlier, in the test center's parking lot and lobby, and Kylara walked in on exam day having never seen the building. One of them took the exam. The other took the exam plus the room.

9.1 What the Room Took

The following are composite cases.

Case A

Revel's reconnaissance visit produced a one-page environmental report in her own shorthand. The lobby check-in involved a metal detector wand and a palm scan, both of which she practiced consenting to in her head for three weeks until neither was news. The waiting area had a wall-mounted television with rolling captions; she noted the seat that faced away from it. The testing room, glimpsed when a staff member kindly opened the door, had overhead fluorescents with a visible flicker at the far end and quieter LED panels near the proctor station. Her accommodation letter already granted a separate room, but the recon told her what to ask for if the separate room fell through: near seat, away from the flickering bank. On the day, the separate room did fall through for the first 20 minutes due to a staffing gap. She sat in her scouted seat, earplugs in, and lost almost nothing, because the fallback had been chosen in advance by a calm version of her rather than improvised by a flooded one.

Case B

Kylara's day began accumulating cost at the door. The wand search was unexpected and set off a wave of tactile alarm that took, by her estimate, half an hour to fully recede. The assigned seat placed a heating vent's whine directly behind her right ear, and she spent the first section deciding whether asking to move would cost more than enduring; she endured. By the halfway point the whine, the flicker, and the scratch of a neighboring candidate's scratch paper had become a fourth, fifth, and sixth exam section running in parallel. Her question routine, drilled for weeks, degraded exactly the way section 5.3 predicts routines degrade under load. She describes the last hour as reading through glass.

The contrast is not resilience. Both women have run demanding careers on sensory systems that charge them for environments other people do not notice. The contrast is that one of them treated the room as a known adversary with a scouting report, and the other met it as a stranger with unlimited credit.

9.2 The Load Underneath

What happened to Kylara has a mechanism, and naming it precisely is what turns her story from a cautionary tale into a design problem. Autistic adults report sensory hypersensitivity at rates above 90 percent in large samples, and the first-person literature is consistent about the two features that make it costly: intensity, the input registers louder, brighter, sharper than it does for others, and inescapability, distress scales with the inability to leave (MacLennan et al., 2022; Robertson & Simmons, 2013). A test room is close to a purpose-built inescapability machine. You cannot move freely, cannot leave without cost, cannot control light, sound, or neighbors, and are being watched, which for many autistic adults is itself a sensory-adjacent channel with its own price.

The cost is paid in the currency the exam runs on. Processing unwanted input, suppressing responses to it, and monitoring it for change all draw on the same limited attentional and working memory resources that question-answering needs (Baddeley, 2012; Eysenck et al., 2007). ADHD nervous systems pay a parallel bill through distractibility: input that autistic candidates experience as painful, ADHD candidates often experience as magnetic, every keyboard click a hook pulling attention off the stem it was holding. AuDHD candidates get both invoices. None of this appears in any score report, and all of it is score.

The design conclusion follows directly. Sensory strategy is not comfort planning, and treating it as pampering is how prepared candidates fail exams they knew. It is load management for the machine taking the test, and it has three layers: the formal layer secured through Chapter 7.0's process, the informal layer arranged through ordinary requests and choices, and the in-seat layer you carry in yourself when the first two leak. The rest of this chapter builds the layers, then pressure-tests them against the format where the room is your own home and somehow still not yours.

9.3 The Three Layers Built

The formal layer was Chapters 6.0 and 7.0's work, so here it needs only its sensory-specific notes. A separate or distraction-reduced room is the highest-value single accommodation for this profile and should be requested wherever functional evidence supports it. Comfort aid lists, the published inventories of items permitted without prior approval, vary by vendor and typically include foam earplugs, certain noise-reducing devices at staff discretion, and small unobtrusive items; anything not listed needs written pre-approval, and the difference between "in my pocket, permitted" and "argued about at the desk at 7:55 a.m." is a difference you settle by email weeks earlier. Meeka's needs-description method from section 7.4 is the route for anything the menu lacks: first-slot scheduling, agreed check-in scripts, seat placement, written notice of procedural changes.

The informal layer costs nothing but foresight. Reconnaissance, Revel's 90 minutes, converts the room from stranger to known quantity, and where a physical visit is impractical, the vendor's published walkthrough videos and candidate forums recover part of the value. Booking choices are sensory choices: the first slot of the morning buys an empty waiting area, a quieter room, and a nervous system that has not spent hours anticipating; midweek dates buy thinner crowds. Clothing is equipment, chosen for the candidate's own known tactile tolerances and the certainty of an unpredictable room temperature, layers being the only strategy that survives both outcomes. And the polite in-room request, may I move seats, could that door be closed, is available to everyone, costs one sentence, and is exercised by almost no one; Kylara's endurance calculation, that asking might cost more than the vent, is the single most common unforced error in this readership's test-day accounts.

The in-seat layer is what remains when both outer layers leak, and it should be built and rehearsed, not improvised. Its contents are unglamorous: a slow-exhale breathing pattern practiced until it is boring, because extended exhalation is the most portable downshift the physiology offers; a pre-chosen anchor action, feet flat, palms on thighs, one full breath, that marks the reset between sections or after a spike; permitted pressure and fidget outlets scaled to what the room allows, a thumb pressed into a palm being invisible and always legal; and the triage rule from section 5.2 extended to sensation, name it, rate it, decide once whether to act, then return to the stem, because the alternative is Kylara's parallel exam of continuous re-deciding. Rehearsal is the load-bearing word. Every element goes into the full-length practice tests of Chapter 10.0's dress rehearsal, under fatigue, until the sequence runs without being summoned.

9.4 The Proctored Screen

The following account is a composite, with details changed for anonymity.

Laker chose online proctoring for his project management certification for exactly the reasons the format advertises: his own room, his own chair, his own lighting, no strangers, no commute. The sensory logic seemed unanswerable, and for candidates whose primary drains are crowds, travel, and unfamiliar spaces, it often is. What Laker had not priced was what the format takes back.

The check-in required a webcam tour of his desk, walls, and under-surfaces, conducted by chat instruction, and ran 40 minutes past the scheduled start, a delay entirely outside his control during which he was required to remain seated and on camera. The exam rules prohibited reading aloud, one of his core processing strategies from his Chapter 2.0 profile, prohibited looking away from the screen for sustained periods, and treated standing or excessive movement as flaggable events. Twenty minutes in, his internet connection hiccuped, the session locked pending reconnection, and he spent the recovery interval watching a spinner and rehearsing catastrophes. He passed, narrowly, and his afterword is the section's thesis: the format had removed every stressor he knew he had and installed a new set, being surveilled, being still, being silent, being at the mercy of a connection, that his profile was worse equipped for, not better.

The decision rule that falls out of Laker's case is profile-matching, not format loyalty. Online proctoring suits candidates whose top drains are environmental and social and whose profiles tolerate stillness, silence, and being watched. It punishes candidates who regulate through movement and vocalization, who find surveillance itself a sensory channel, or whose anxiety amplifies under technical uncertainty. The room it offers is yours, but the rules inside it are not, and a candidate choosing between formats should read the specific vendor's proctoring conduct rules as carefully as the syllabus, then choose the room whose taxes their own profile can best afford. Movement-based accommodations, for the record, can be requested for online formats too, permission to stand, to read aloud, to look away, and almost nobody knows to ask.

9.5 What to Carry Forward

Kylara resat the exam 11 weeks later. The knowledge work of those weeks was minor revision; the real campaign was everything this chapter has assembled. She visited the center twice, once just to stand in the lobby. Her comfort aid email exchange ran to four messages and ended with named permissions in writing. She booked the first slot on a Tuesday, wore the clothes from her second recon visit, and moved seats on request, one sentence, granted in ten seconds, when she was placed near the vent she already knew by name. Her in-seat sequence had been rehearsed through three full-length practice tests at her kitchen table with a construction crew working next door, which she describes, not entirely joking, as the best accommodation money couldn't buy. She passed with 14 minutes to spare, a 23 point swing on a knowledge base that had barely moved.

The room did not change between her two attempts. The building, the wand, the vent, and the flicker were all faithfully at their posts. What changed is that the second time, the room had already been taken before the exam began, scouted, negotiated with, dressed for, and rehearsed against, and so the only thing left to take on the day was the test. That is the whole strategy, and Chapter 10.0 extends it from the room to the 72 hours that deliver you into it.

Chapter 10.0: The 72 Hour Protocol

What is the highest-scoring thing a candidate can do in the last three days before a professional exam? Ask the question in any study group and the answers arrive in one flavor: final reviews, weak-area blitzes, one more full practice test, cramming defended as consolidation. Ask the performance literature instead and the answer is almost insultingly different. In the final 72 hours, the marginal value of new knowledge approaches zero, while the marginal value of sleep, medication stability, decision reduction, and arousal management approaches its maximum. The last three days are not the last three days of studying. They are the first three days of the exam, and the candidates who treat them that way are playing a different, easier game.

10.1 The Problem With the Final Push

The instinct to push hardest at the end has a mechanism behind it, and for this readership the mechanism is a trap with teeth. Deadline urgency is the one reliable recruiter of ADHD attention, so the final days deliver the focus that the previous months rationed, and spending it feels not just natural but overdue, like finally being the student you meant to be. The push then collects its price in the room. Late-night cramming trades sleep for material, and the sleep research is unambiguous about the direction of that trade: restriction degrades sustained attention, working memory, and processing speed, the exact substrate the exam taxes, and consolidation of what was learned depends on the sleep being sacrificed (Lim & Dinges, 2010; Walker, 2017). Executive systems already running on impaired budgets degrade first and furthest. The candidate arrives with three more facts and 20 fewer IQ points' worth of function, having paid premium hours for negative return.

The final push also breaks things that were working. New material encountered at the end has a documented tendency to feel more urgent than it is, spawning last-minute strategy changes, a new guessing rule read on a forum, a reorganized noteboard scheme, an untested morning routine, each one a deviation from rehearsed process at the exact moment rehearsal was supposed to pay off. And for candidates prescribed stimulant medication, the final push era is when the worst pharmacological ideas arrive: the skipped dose to sleep longer, the doubled dose to focus harder, the borrowed strategy from someone else's prescription. Every one of those is a live experiment run for the first time on the highest-stakes day of the year.

So the problem, stated as concretely as the archetype demands: the last 72 hours reliably convert prepared candidates into impaired ones, through mechanisms their own neurotype makes more seductive, and no amount of content mastery defends against it. The defense has to be structural. It has to be a protocol, written in advance, boring by design, and rehearsed like everything else in this book.

10.2 What Failed Before the Protocol

The following account is a composite, with details changed for anonymity.

Firdous failed her pharmacy licensure exam twice before anyone looked at her final week instead of her knowledge. Attempt one followed the classic arc: question-bank scores climbing nicely until ten days out, then a panic audit that convinced her she was behind, then four nights averaging five hours of sleep, the last of them spent re-deriving calculation formulas until 2 a.m. She describes sitting down at the terminal feeling like her head was full of wet sand. Attempt two was supposed to fix this, and the fix made it stranger: she took the day before entirely off, on advice, but the vacuum filled itself. With no plan for the empty day, she spent it refreshing a candidates' forum, absorbing other people's panic and a rumor about a changed question format that turned out to be false, and slept four hours on adrenaline and dread. Her practice-test average across both campaigns would have passed comfortably. Twice, the person who showed up was not the person who had earned that average.

The pattern in Firdous's two failures is the chapter's pivot. Attempt one failed on load, the final push spending the resources the exam needed. Attempt two failed on vacuum, rest declared but not designed, leaving a nervous system alone with unstructured time and a phone. The correction is not more rest or more work. It is that the final 72 hours must be scheduled with the same specificity as any exam section, hour by hour, decided in advance by the calm version of the candidate, so that the anxious version has nothing left to decide.

10.3 The Protocol Itself

The protocol below is a template to be filled from your Chapter 2.0 profile, not a prescription. Its logic is fixed; its contents are yours.

Seventy-two to 48 hours out is the last window containing anything resembling study, and it is retrieval-only at low volume: a final pass through a small, pre-chosen error deck, no new material under any circumstances, no full practice tests, which at this range cost arousal and sleep for information you can no longer act on. The decision freeze begins here, a written rule that no strategy, no schedule element, and no medication arrangement changes from this point, whatever any forum says. Logistics complete today: documents and permitted items staged by the door against the vendor's published list, route rehearsed, accommodation letters printed twice, clothing chosen. If the center was never scouted, this is the last responsible moment for the parking-lot visit.

Forty-eight to 24 hours out is the dress rehearsal of the morning, not the exam: wake at exam-day time, run the exact breakfast, medication timing, and departure sequence, then spend the day at deliberately low cognitive load, structured hour by hour, the structure being the entire point. Movement helps most profiles here, familiar and moderate rather than novel and exhausting. The error deck may make one final short appearance if idleness is intolerable; for many candidates it should not. Screens get a curfew. Sleep protection tonight matters more than tomorrow's, since night-before sleep is often poor regardless, and the research consolation is real: one bad final night on top of a well-slept week is survivable, while a badly slept week is not (Walker, 2017).

The final 24 hours run on rails laid earlier. No study, full stop; the marginal fact now costs more than it pays. The evening script is written and boring, the same meal that has worked before, the bag by the door untouched since yesterday, a wind-down sequence rehearsed during the practice-test weeks so that tonight it signals normality rather than emergency. In-bed rumination gets a pre-assigned tool: the expressive-writing result, in which ten minutes spent writing worries down before a test measurably improved performance among anxious testers, is one of the few interventions cheap enough and evidenced enough to earn a place in the final hours (Ramirez & Beilock, 2011). The morning runs the rehearsed sequence to the minute, arrives early to a scouted building, deploys the sensory kit of Chapter 9.0, and reframes the inevitable arousal in the doorway with the one-line reappraisal the evidence supports: this is the body arriving ready, and performance under "I am excited" reliably beats performance under "I must calm down" (Brooks, 2014).

Medication holds a fenced place in all three days, and the fence has one rule: the exam period runs on the regimen your prescriber set, exactly as prescribed, with any exam-specific timing questions, covering a 5 p.m. finish on an 8 a.m. dose, for instance, raised with the prescriber weeks earlier, not solved in the kitchen at dawn. Stimulant effects on cognition are real and are the reason consistency matters (Cortese et al., 2018; Advokat, 2010); they are also dose-experienced and person-specific, which is precisely why exam week is the worst possible laboratory. The protocol's position is absolute where the evidence and the stakes agree: no first-time doses, no skipped doses, no borrowed strategies, nothing new on the day.

10.4 The Protocol Under Fire

The following worked example uses a composite case.

Zebedee, sitting a structural engineering licensure exam, wrote his protocol five weeks out and rehearsed its morning sequence twice during full-length practice tests. The value of that paperwork revealed itself when his 72 hours went wrong in three separate places.

Step 1: The Thursday disruption

At 71 hours out, his employer called an emergency site inspection for the following afternoon, deleting the center of his 48-hour day. The protocol's written contingency line, any disrupted block moves to its backup slot, unchanged in content, meant the low-load afternoon became a low-load evening, and, critically, the deleted hours were not backfilled with study. He reports the strong pull to treat the disruption as license to cram, and the written rule as the only thing that outvoted it.

Step 2: The forum grenade

At 30 hours out, a study-group message claimed the afternoon session's reference handbook had changed editions. The decision freeze held: the rule said no strategy changes on unverified information, and the verification path, the vendor's official page, took four minutes to show the claim was wrong. Zebedee's note afterward is worth quoting to every candidate: the freeze did not stop the anxiety, it just gave the anxiety nowhere to go.

Step 3: The three a.m. audit

The night before, he woke at 3:10 a.m. with his mind running failure arithmetic. The pre-assigned tool was on the nightstand: pen, pad, ten minutes of writing the worries out, lights back off. He estimates he slept another three hours. The morning sequence then ran on rails precisely because it had been rehearsed twice; he describes executing it "like a checklist, feeling nothing, which was the point."

The complicating moment

One element failed outright. His plan assumed medication at 6:30 a.m. would cover the full day; the afternoon session found him flat and drifting, a timing question he had never raised with his prescriber because it had never mattered on practice days half as long. He passed regardless, on margin built elsewhere, and his first post-exam action was booking the prescriber conversation for the retake he turned out not to need. The lesson stands as the section's closing point: the protocol handles what was rehearsed, and its gaps are exactly the conversations you did not have early enough.

10.5 Settling the Account

The verdict a senior colleague would deliver on all this is short. Your last 72 hours are an operations problem, and you already know how to solve operations problems: in writing, in advance, with backups. So write the protocol at least a month out, while you are calm and it is theoretical. Freeze decisions from three days; retrieval-only from 72 hours; nothing at all from 24. Rehearse the morning twice inside full-length practice tests, because a sequence rehearsed is a sequence that runs under fire. Fence the medication regimen and hold the prescriber conversations weeks early, covering timing against the exam's actual length. Give the night-before mind its pen and pad. And accept, in advance, that something in the three days will go wrong, an employer, a forum, a 3 a.m. audit, because the protocol's real product is not a perfect run-in. It is a candidate for whom the disruption has a pre-written answer, which is the only kind of candidate disruption cannot bill.

What the protocol delivers to the door, Chapter 9.0's layers protect inside the room, and for most written exams that completes the campaign. Two formats, though, add an examiner watching your hands and a clock on your talking, and they need their own chapter.

Chapter 11.0: Performance and Practical Exams

The buzzer sounded and Louka stepped through the curtain into station four. A plastic mannequin lay on the bed, an examiner stood in the corner with a clipboard, and a laminated card on the trolley described a scenario she had 15 minutes to manage. She had performed this exact skill perhaps four hundred times on real patients. What she had never done was perform it while narrating every action aloud, to a silent stranger scoring her against criteria she could not see, with a countdown clock in her peripheral vision and the previous station's fumbled reading still replaying in the back of her head. Her hands knew the work. The format was the stranger.

11.1 The Station in Full

Louka is a composite, details changed for anonymity, and her exam was an OSCE, the **objective structured clinical examination** format that internationally trained nurses face at UK regulator test centers, that medical, dental, pharmacy, and physician associate candidates meet in their own versions, and that has cousins across the trades wherever a practical test puts an assessor's eyes on a candidate's hands (Khan et al., 2013; Nursing and Midwifery Council, 2021). The format's architecture is a circuit: timed stations, buzzer transitions, a scenario card at each door, standardized patients or mannequins inside, and examiners scoring observable behaviors against structured criteria.

Her first attempt failed three stations of 16, and the pattern of the three failures is the chapter's syllabus. Station four she failed on narration: she performed the skill correctly and silently, and criteria she could not demonstrate through observable behavior went unscored; the format wanted her working memory to run the skill and a commentary channel simultaneously, and under load the commentary channel shut down. Station nine she failed on a reading error, misparsing one clause of a dense scenario card in the 60 seconds allotted, an error Chapter 5.0 would have predicted to the sentence. Station 12 she failed on the transition: station 11 had gone badly, the buzzer gave her 20 seconds to reset, and she carried the previous failure through the curtain into a task that then received perhaps 70 percent of her attention. Her clinical knowledge was never the problem. Sixteen consecutive context switches, under observation, against dense text, with no recovery time, was a format aimed, with no malice and considerable precision, at every expensive feature of her profile at once.

11.2 Why This Format Bites Harder

Name the mechanisms and the design problem clarifies. The OSCE circuit is a transition engine, and section 4.5 established what transitions cost monotropic attention; 16 stations is 16 forced disengagements and re-engagements, each one taxed. The observation is a second exam running in parallel: performing under evaluative eyes recruits the masking machinery autistic adults describe as their most expensive subsystem (Hull et al., 2017), and the pressure-degrades-performance literature shows skilled performance breaking down precisely when self-monitoring is amplified, the mechanism Beilock's work made famous as choking, attention turning inward onto processes that run better unwatched (Beilock, 2010). The narration demand splits working memory between doing and describing, a dual task that punishes anyone whose verbal channel and motor channel compete rather than cooperate. The scenario cards are Chapter 5.0's dense stems with a 60 second clock. And the interpersonal stations, standardized patients performing distress, examiners offering nothing, ask autistic candidates to read staged social signals under time pressure, a task the double empathy literature would flag as measuring something other than clinical competence (Milton, 2012).

One legal boundary from section 6.2 governs everything that follows, and practical formats are where it actually bites. Adjustments may change how competence is demonstrated, never what competence is. A regulator cannot waive the requirement to safely perform the skill, manage the deteriorating patient, or communicate critical information, because those are the competence standard itself. What sits around the standard, the reading time for cards, the transition intervals, the sensory environment, the advance disclosure of procedure, rest breaks across a long circuit, is adjustable, and candidates routinely fail to request adjustments there because the format's untouchable core convinces them the whole thing is untouchable. The design work of this chapter lives exactly in that adjustable perimeter.

11.3 Training for the Format

The following are composite cases.

Case A

Huxon prepared for his practical welding inspection exam the way this book prepares for everything: by rehearsing the format until the format stopped being information. He built a station simulator in his garage, timed cards, a kitchen timer standing in for the buzzer, and drafted his partner to stand silently with a clipboard, a presence he reports was absurd for one evening and then simply true. His narration training borrowed a coaching structure: perform the skill silently, then narrating, then narrating while the timer ran, adding one load per week. For transitions he built a 20 second reset ritual, clipboard down, one slow exhale, feet planted, next card, and drilled it between simulated stations until the ritual, not the rumination, was what the buzzer triggered. He passed with examiner comments noting his communication, the channel that had never once been his strength, and his summary earns its place in the chapter: the skill was never the exam, the format was the exam, so I trained the format.

Case B

Colbee trained for the same certification with equal diligence pointed at the wrong target: content and skill repetitions, hundreds of them, all solo, all silent, all untimed. His first attempt failed on the same three mechanisms as Louka's, narration collapse, a card misread, a carried failure. The instructive part is the second attempt, because Colbee could not replicate Huxon's home simulation, no partner, no space, and built substitutes instead: narration drilled into a phone camera, which supplied a surprising fraction of the observed-performance pressure; transitions drilled at a public gym, using machine changeovers as buzzers; card reading drilled with Chapter 5.0's ask-first routine against a 60 second timer. He also requested, and received, printed cards in a larger font and a first-in-circuit start time, perimeter adjustments he had not known existed until he asked the needs-description question from section 7.4. He passed the resit. The contrast with Huxon is not resources but aim, and the two cases together make the section's rule: whatever fraction of the format you can simulate, simulate, and request adjustments for the fraction you cannot.

11.4 The Adjustable Perimeter

The requestable items for observed and practical formats deserve their own inventory, because almost no published accommodation menu is written with this format in mind, and every item below has been granted somewhere by a major testing body operating under the frameworks of Chapter 6.0.

Time adjustments translate differently here: rather than more minutes inside a station, which can distort standardized scenarios, bodies more readily grant extended reading time before stations, longer transition intervals, and scheduled rest breaks across the circuit, each of which targets a mechanism from section 11.2 directly. Procedural disclosure is the sleeper request: a written walkthrough of the day's choreography, the check-in, the circuit order, the buzzer conventions, what examiners will and will not say, costs the body nothing and removes the unpredictability tax that autistic candidates pay heaviest; Meeka's method from section 7.4 is the route. Sensory items carry over from Chapter 9.0 intact, with one format-specific addition: requesting a consistent examiner briefing so that permitted self-regulation, movement, fidget items, brief eye-contact breaks, is not misread live as incompetence or distress. And communication-channel adjustments, written rather than verbal station instructions, permission to ask for one repetition of verbal information, exist and are granted, sitting just inside the perimeter provided the competence standard itself does not test the channel in question.

The request logic is identical to Chapter 7.0's, with one addition of emphasis: link every item to a mechanism, not a diagnosis. A file that says autistic candidates need predictability will lose to a file that says this candidate's documented processing profile means unexpected procedural change measurably degrades performance, and a written schedule removes the distortion without touching the standard. Reviewers of practical exams are guarding the competence standard with justified vigilance. Requests framed as protecting the measurement, which is what they genuinely are, recruit that vigilance instead of fighting it.

11.5 From Theory to Practice

Louka's resit, five months later, is the chapter run as a checklist. Her simulator was a church hall, a friend, and a set of laminated cards she made herself. Narration was trained on the graduated ladder until the commentary channel survived full load. Every card got the ask-first reading routine, drilled at 60 seconds. The reset ritual was rehearsed until the buzzer triggered it unbidden. Her requests, submitted through the regulator's process with her assessor's mechanism-linked letter, came back granting extended card-reading time, a written procedural walkthrough, and a scheduled mid-circuit break. Stations still went wrong; one mannequin scenario drifted somewhere her rehearsals had never been, and she scored it poorly. What did not happen is the cascade. The reset ritual spent its 20 seconds, station 13 received a whole candidate, and the circuit ended with 14 of 16 stations passed and the credential secured.

The theory of this whole book, profile, then system, then rehearsal, then perimeter, is nowhere more literal than here, where the exam finally stops being a document and becomes a room with your body in it. The format can be trained because the format is finite. The perimeter can be adjusted because the law says so. And the skill, the thing you actually came to demonstrate, was yours before the buzzer and stays yours after. Chapter 12.0 handles the day the letter comes back, whichever letter it is.

Chapter 12.0: Results, Retakes, and Recovery

A candidate who had just failed a licensure exam for the second time told her study group something that stuck with everyone in the thread: the score report took her four days to open, and when she finally read it, the number was survivable, but the week she had spent imagining it nearly wasn't. She had failed by eight points and spent four days grieving a catastrophe her mind had scored at minus two hundred. The gap between those two numbers, the result and the felt result, is where retake campaigns are won and lost, and for this readership the gap runs wider than for anyone else in the room.

12.1 The Problem With Failing

Start with the base rates, because shame does its best work in the dark. Professional exams fail people routinely: first-attempt pass rates on major licensure exams commonly run between 60 and 85 percent, retake candidates pass at lower but substantial rates, and every regulator's statistics quietly describe a system in which failing an attempt is an ordinary event experienced by enormous numbers of eventually licensed professionals. The exam is designed to be failable. That is what makes passing it mean anything.

For neurodivergent candidates, though, an ordinary event lands on extraordinary wiring. The ADHD literature documents emotion dysregulation as a core-adjacent feature of the condition: emotional responses that arrive faster, run hotter, and take longer to discharge than the situation licenses (Shaw et al., 2014; Barkley, 2015). The community's name for the sharpest edge of this, rejection sensitive dysphoria, describes the disproportionate, sometimes physical pain of perceived failure and rejection; the term comes from clinical description rather than validated instruments, and the honest position is that the label remains informal while the dysregulation it points at is thoroughly documented. Add the biographical load, decades of underperformance relative to effort, school reports that read as character indictments, the compensation history of section 1.4, and a failed exam does not arrive as information. It arrives as a verdict confirming the oldest file the candidate keeps on themselves. The autistic contribution stacks on top: a failed attempt often collapses a painstakingly built routine and certainty structure, and post-failure shutdown or burnout can take the study system offline entirely (Raymaker et al., 2020).

The problem, stated concretely: the days after a failed result are when retake campaigns are actually decided, and this readership meets those days with a nervous system that turns an eight point gap into an identity event. Every early attempt to solve this with information, the base rates, the pep talks, fails for a reason the next section owns.

12.2 What Does Not Work

The instinctive responses to a failed result form their own graveyard, and walking it briefly saves the reader from digging fresh plots.

Immediate rebooking fails most often. It feels like resilience, cancel the grief by scheduling the redemption, and it books a retake before the forensics of section 12.3 have identified what actually went wrong, guaranteeing the same campaign runs again against the same wall. The eligibility clock makes this worse: many boards impose waiting periods and attempt limits, and a panic rebooking can spend a limited attempt on an unchanged candidate.

The pure willpower narrative fails quietly. Study harder, want it more, treats the result as a motivation deficit, and Chapter 1.0 spent its whole length on why that diagnosis is wrong; applied post-failure it adds shame to a system already flooded with it, and shame, section 1.3 established, is fuel for avoidance, not effort.

And the opposite move, the permanent quiet withdrawal, fails invisibly. Nobody announces it. The candidate simply does not rebook, the emails go unopened, and a career door closes without a decision ever being made. The withdrawal is the emotion dysregulation completing its arc unopposed, and it is common enough that regulators' own data show meaningful populations of candidates with remaining attempts who never return. Distinguishing this from its healthy cousin, the strategic pause, is a design problem this chapter takes up in section 12.4, because from the inside, in week one, they feel identical.

12.3 The Pivot Is Sequencing

The following account is a composite, with details changed for anonymity.

Bowden failed his commercial certification by 11 points and did, in order, everything the graveyard contains: rebooked within 48 hours, studied harder inside his unchanged system, burned out at week five, and let the rebooked date lapse unattended, which cost him the fee and very nearly the candidacy. What rebuilt him was a sequence a mentor imposed, and the sequence, not any single element in it, is the pivot this chapter turns on: first aid, then forensics, then design, then commitment, in that order, with each stage gated behind the previous one.

First aid came first and contained no exam content whatsoever. Seventy-two hours in which the result was allowed to be what it was, the people who needed telling were told in one sentence with no autopsy attached, sleep and food and movement were treated as the actual tasks, and the score report stayed closed. The expressive writing tool from section 10.3 did its second job of the campaign here. Self-compassion in this stage is not decoration; the research base associates it with better recovery from failure and, counterintuitively to every shame-driven instinct, with more retake motivation rather than less (Neff, 2003; Gilbert, 2009).

Forensics opened only when the first aid had discharged enough voltage that the score report could be read as data. Bowden's report, like most, localized the damage: two domains carried the failure, and his time data showed a collapse in the final section. The forensic question set is the same five-way sort every failed attempt deserves, because each cause routes to a different chapter of this book: a knowledge gap routes to Chapters 3.0 and 4.0; a timing and format failure routes to Chapter 5.0; a regulation failure, the flooding, the freeze, routes to Chapters 9.0 and 10.0; an environment failure routes to Chapter 9.0's layers and the accommodation file; an administrative failure, the unapplied-for adjustment, the missed deadline, routes to Chapters 2.0 and 7.0. Bowden's sort came out two parts knowledge, one part timing collapse, and zero parts the character indictment he had spent week one writing.

Design and commitment then followed as engineering rather than penance: the retake campaign rebuilt around the forensic findings, the minimum viable session reinstated, the timing routine drilled at full length, and the new date chosen against the eligibility calendar and his actual readiness rather than against the shame clock. He passed the third attempt by 14 points. The sequence is the teaching: every element existed in earlier chapters, and only the ordering was new.

12.4 The Harder Sort

The following is a composite case; identifying details have been changed.

Background

Yonatan, a 44 year old candidate for a clinical licensure exam, presented a harder version of the post-failure problem. The failed attempt was his third, his jurisdiction allowed one more, and the failure had arrived during a period of genuine autistic burnout following a workplace restructure. He had begun, in his words, to suspect the honest answer was that he could not do this, and he wanted help distinguishing that conclusion from the avoidance he knew his history contained.

Presentation

He described a study system that had actually held, forensics that showed narrow knowledge gaps but a broad regulation collapse across the exam day, exhaustion that predated the attempt by months, and a strong pull toward both immediate rebooking and permanent withdrawal on alternating days.

Analysis

The distinction he was asking for has real criteria. A strategic pause is chosen against named conditions: it has a review date, it names what must change before resumption, burnout recovery, an accommodation appeal, a life logistics change, and it protects the candidacy, tracking eligibility windows and documentation currency during the pause. Avoidance-in-progress has none of these; it is open-ended, condition-free, and lets deadlines lapse by silence. The fourth-attempt scarcity made the sort higher stakes but did not change the criteria. His regulation-collapse forensics, meanwhile, argued that an unchanged retake would spend the final attempt on the least-changed variable.

Intervention

The plan was a structured pause with teeth: six months, a review date in the calendar and in two other people's calendars, burnout recovery treated as the primary project on the evidence that it, not knowledge, had failed, the accommodation file rebuilt in month four using Chapter 7.0's method to add the rest breaks and separate room his first three attempts had never had, and a written resumption threshold he drafted himself, specifying the sleep, capacity, and practice-test markers that would greenlight booking.

Outcome

He resumed at month seven, one month late against the plan and by agreement rather than by drift, and passed the fourth attempt with the rebuilt accommodations in place. He has said since that the pause was the attempt, and the exam merely confirmed it. Not every version of this case ends with a license; some end with a chosen redirection, and the criteria above are what make such an ending a decision rather than a disappearance.

Teaching Points

- A pause is strategic when it has conditions, dates, and witnesses; it is avoidance when it has none.
- Forensics that blame regulation or burnout argue for changing the candidate's conditions, not for spending scarce attempts faster.
- Protecting eligibility and documentation during a pause is what keeps a pause reversible.

12.5 Money, Windows, and the Long Game

The unglamorous variables deserve one clear-eyed section, because they decide more retake campaigns than motivation does. Attempts cost money, resit fees, travel, sometimes fresh documentation, and a candidate budgeting a campaign should price two attempts from the start, not as pessimism but as the same insurance thinking that prices a spare tire. Eligibility windows are the harder currency: authorization periods that expire, waiting intervals between attempts, attempt limits per window or per lifetime, and education-currency rules that can force expensive refreshers if a candidacy lapses. Every one of these belongs on the Chapter 2.0 administrative map from the first day of the first campaign, with the same externalization rules, because the cruelest version of the post-failure story is the candidate who recovered, rebuilt, and discovered the window had closed while they were healing.

The long game frame is the one this readership is owed after everything the previous chapters have asked of it. A professional exam is one gate in a long career, and the license, once earned, does not carry an asterisk recording the attempts. The skills this book has actually been teaching, profiling your own machine, building systems that survive your worst weeks, extracting adjustments from institutions, running protocols under fire, and sorting failure into fixable parts, are not exam skills that expire at the test center door. They are the operating manual for a neurodivergent professional career, and the exam merely forced their development on a deadline.

12.6 Looking Back and Ahead

Return to the candidate from the opening, the one whose score report sat unopened for four days while an imagined catastrophe collected interest. Her thread, it turns out, had a second post, written months later, that the study group quoted long after she had passed: the failure cost me eight points, and the story I told about the failure cost me a month, and only one of those was on the syllabus.

That is this chapter compressed, and in a sense the whole book. The result is data; the felt result is weather; and the sequence, first aid before forensics, forensics before design, design before commitment, is how a candidate keeps the weather from voting on the data. What she did next, the five-way sort, the rebuilt campaign, the date chosen by readiness rather than shame, you now hold in full. What she could not have known, and what you now do, is that none of it needed to be improvised in the worst week. It could all have been written down in advance, by the calm version of her, in a book like this one, waiting for a day she hoped never to need it. The conclusion that follows closes the loop on that idea, because there is one last thing the license will not do for you, and it is worth saying plainly before you go.

Conclusion

Licensed, not cured. That is the honest label for what waits on the other side of the exam, and it is worth a moment before the book lets you go, because the exam preparation genre likes to end on transformation and this book has no intention of starting to lie in its final pages.

The credential you are working toward will change your title, your scope of practice, and in most cases your income and your options. It will not change your attention system, your sensory profile, your decoding speed, or your executive function. Morag passed her boards and still cannot open a question bank at 9 p.m. Ledger holds his license and still reads at Ledger speed. Yonatan practices under the credential he nearly abandoned, and his capacity still has the limits that the burnout year taught him to respect. The machine you mapped in Chapter 2.0 is the machine you will run your career on.

Here is why that is good news rather than the consolation prize it sounds like. Everything you built to get through the gate was built for that machine, and none of it expires at the test center door. The minimum viable session that survived your worst weeks is a continuing education system now. The question attack routine is how you will read dense regulatory updates for the next 30 years. The accommodation file, current and well built, is a workplace adjustments request waiting to be re-addressed. The 72 hour protocol is every high-stakes presentation, audit, and inspection day for the rest of your working life. The failure forensics are how you will handle the setbacks a career reliably supplies. You did not just prepare for an exam. You reverse-engineered yourself, under pressure, on a deadline, and wrote the manual.

Two smaller things, and then the door. First, the system you fought through is still under construction, and it improves the way it has always improved: by candidates using it, appealing it, and leaving the paperwork trail that moves the next review toward yes. Every well-built request you file makes the machinery slightly more literate in profiles like yours. You do not owe anyone activism. But if you ever wonder whether engaging the process matters beyond your own result, the history in Chapter 6.0 already answered.

Second, somewhere behind you on this road is a candidate who is currently in week three of a collapsed study calendar, concluding that they are not a test taker. You were told the truth in Chapter 1.0 and it held all the way here: the plan was scored by ambition when it should have been scored by survivability, and nothing about them needs to change except the engineering. When you meet that person, and in a licensed career you will, you now know exactly what to hand them.

Go take the exam. The door was always going to open to the version of you that stopped trying to be someone else on the way through it.

Appendix A: The Campaign Timeline

This appendix compresses the whole book into one backward-planned calendar. Work from your exam date, or your target exam window if no date is booked, and place each milestone against it. Where your testing body's published deadlines are stricter than the defaults here, the testing body wins. Verify every deadline directly with your exam program before relying on this or any template.

Six or more months out

- Identify the decision desk for accommodations: board, vendor, or agency (section 7.1). One phone call or email settles it.
- Read the program's documentation guideline in full and note the recency requirement for assessments.
- Inventory your evidence: diagnostic reports, school records, university support letters, workplace adjustment emails, prior exam accommodations (section 7.2).
- If documentation is stale or absent, book the assessment now. Waiting lists are the timeline's most common killer.
- Begin the two week observation period for your Chapter 2.0 profile.

Five months out

- Complete and freeze the one page profile.
- Write the clinician briefing sheet (Appendix B) and deliver it before your assessment appointment.
- Build the study system skeleton: minimum viable session defined in writing, anchor chosen, flat restart rule and bonus clause written down (section 3.3).
- Start the question bank. The bank is the campaign's center from week one, not a final month add-on (section 4.3).

Four months out

- Submit the accommodation application to the correct desk. Confirm receipt in writing and diary the program's stated review period.
- Put every date from this appendix on a wall calendar and in one other person's calendar (section 2.4).

Three months out

- Chase the application if the stated review period has lapsed. Polite, written, dated.
- If denied: run the appeal sequence in Chapter 8.0 immediately and ask about deadline extensions pending appeal.
- First full length timed practice test, run under exam conditions, including your question attack routine and in seat sensory sequence.

Two months out

- On approval: book the accommodated seat through the specified channel. Accommodated seats need more lead time and fewer venues offer them (section 7.3).
- Reconnaissance visit to the test center, or the online proctoring system check if testing remotely (sections 9.3 and 9.4).
- Settle comfort aid permissions by email. Save the reply.
- Raise medication timing questions with your prescriber, matched to the exam's actual length and start time (section 10.3).

One month out

- Write the 72 hour protocol (Appendix E). Rehearse the exam morning sequence inside a full length practice test.
- Second full length practice test at realistic fatigue, with triage and reset rituals running.
- Confirm the booking, the accommodation letter, and the venue's copy of both.

Final two weeks

- Taper new material to zero. Retrieval only, from a shrinking error deck.
- Third and final full length rehearsal no later than ten days out.
- Stage documents and permitted items. Rehearse the route.

Final 72 hours

- Run Appendix E exactly as written. Nothing new on the day.

Appendix B: The Clinician Briefing Sheet

Assessors are experts in conditions, not in your exam. This one page brief aims their expertise at the document the reviewer actually needs (section 7.2). Copy the structure, fill it in plain language, and hand it over before the appointment. You are not telling the clinician what to conclude. You are telling them what the conclusion must speak to.

1. The exam. Name, awarding body, format (multiple choice, essay, practical stations), total duration, number of questions or stations, and whether it is computer based, paper based, or observed practical.

2. The documentation standard. Attach or summarize the program's published guideline. Note the recency requirement, any named required tests or measures, and the requirement (nearly universal) that reports state current functional limitation and recommend specific accommodations in specific quantities.

3. What the exam demands functionally. Sustained attention for X hours. Reading Y scenario questions of 60 to 120 words each under time pressure. Sitting in a shared room under observation. Rapid transitions between stations. Whatever your exam actually asks of a nervous system, listed plainly.

4. Concrete recent examples of impairment under those demands. Three to six bullet points, specific and dated where possible. A timed practice test where the final section collapsed. A work task under deadline where errors clustered. The reread rate on dense documents. Real incidents beat adjectives.

5. History. Prior accommodations anywhere (school, university, workplace, other exams), with paper if it exists. Where history is thin because diagnosis came late, say so directly and include any early records that describe the impairment without naming it.

6. The requests. The specific accommodations you believe the evidence supports, with quantities: 25 or 50 percent additional time, separate room, rest breaks that stop the clock, reader or text to speech, extended reading time before practical stations, written procedural walkthrough. The clinician's report should recommend, in its own professional judgment, whichever of these the assessment supports, in exactly this level of specificity.

One sentence to remember from section 7.1 while writing it: "would benefit from" loses; "requires, because of the following current limitations" wins.

Appendix C: The Evidence File Checklist

Assemble the file before you need it, in one folder, digital and printed. The reviewer's three questions (section 7.1) are the file's table of contents: covered condition, current functional limitation, logical link to each request.

Core documents, all candidates

- Diagnostic report from an appropriately qualified professional, within the program's recency window where one applies.
- Current functional evidence: the assessor's report addressing this exam's demands (Appendix B output), including standardized measures where the program requires them.
- Personal statement, one page, factual, describing functional impact in daily and testing life. No adjectives doing the work of examples.
- Prior accommodation evidence: school or university support plans, workplace adjustment correspondence, approval letters from any previous high stakes exam. Federal guidance gives past testing accommodations considerable weight; put them on page one of the cover summary.
- Cover summary, one page, listing the requests with quantities and mapping each to its supporting document.

United States additions

- Check whether your program participates in any reciprocity or streamlined route for candidates previously accommodated on major standardized tests, and supply those approval letters if so.
- Keep the Department of Justice testing accommodation guidance in your folder. You will not usually need to cite it. When you do (section 8.3), cite it by name.

- Remember the mitigating measures rule: describe functioning without discounting for medication or coping systems. The law is explicit that these cannot count against coverage.

United Kingdom additions

- Frame requests as reasonable adjustments under the Equality Act 2010; the duty on qualification bodies is anticipatory.
- For specific learning difficulties, many UK bodies expect a diagnostic assessment by a suitably qualified specialist (for dyslexia, commonly a practitioner psychologist or specialist teacher assessor with a current practicing certificate). Check the body's stated standard before booking any assessment.
- Where needs are sensory or procedural rather than time based, use the needs description method (section 7.4): functional facts, mapped to the day's choreography, with an invitation to propose arrangements. Get the agreed arrangements in writing and bring the writing on the day.

File hygiene

- Every submission confirmed by email you can point to later.
- Every deadline in two calendars, one of them not yours.
- Nothing original leaves your hands; copies only.

Appendix D: The Sensory Audit

Complete this before booking, revisit it after reconnaissance, and convert every red item into either a formal request (Chapter 7.0), an informal arrangement (section 9.3), or an in seat plan (section 9.3). The audit's question, from section 2.3: what does your nervous system spend working memory on that other candidates get for free?

Channel by channel. For each channel, note your known triggers, rate the typical cost (low, moderate, high), and mark whether the problem is the stimulus itself or the inability to escape it. The remedy differs (section 2.3).

- Sound: HVAC drone, keyboard clatter, coughing, invigilator movement, timers.
- Light: fluorescent flicker, glare, brightness extremes, screen refresh.
- Touch: chair texture, required lanyards or badges, clothing seams, room temperature swings.
- Smell: cleaning products, other candidates, food smells from waiting areas.
- Visual movement: pacing invigilators, other candidates in peripheral vision, wall clocks.
- Social: being watched, check in interactions, small talk in waiting areas, unexpected instructions delivered verbally.
- Interoceptive: hunger, thirst, needing the bathroom under a no break clock.

The known adversaries list. From reconnaissance (section 9.3), name the specific building's specific problems: the wanding at the door, the television in the waiting area, the vent behind row three. A named adversary can be planned for; an ambush cannot.

The kit. Against the vendor's published comfort aid list, assemble: earplugs of a type you have rehearsed with, layers for temperature, permitted snacks and water for break access, and anything else the list allows that your channels above call for. Anything not on the list gets requested in writing, weeks out.

The in seat sequence. Write yours here and rehearse it inside every full length practice test: the slow exhale pattern, the anchor action, the permitted pressure or fidget outlet, and the one decision rule for mid exam sensory events (name it, rate it, decide once, return to the stem).

Appendix E: The 72 Hour Protocol Template

Write this at least one month out, while calm, and follow it while not. The logic is Chapter 10.0's; the entries are yours. Anything left blank becomes a decision your anxious version will have to make live, which is the failure mode the protocol exists to prevent.

Rules in force from 72 hours (copy verbatim into yours)

- Decision freeze: no strategy, schedule, or medication changes from this point, on any information that has not been verified against the official source.
- No new material. Retrieval only, from the pre chosen error deck, until 24 hours out. Nothing at all after that.
- Medication exactly as prescribed. All timing questions were for the prescriber, weeks ago. Nothing new on the day.
- Any disrupted block moves to its backup slot unchanged in content. Disruption is never license to cram.

Day three (72 to 48 hours)

- Error deck pass: [time, place, deck size]
- Logistics completion: documents and permitted items staged, route rehearsed, accommodation letters printed twice: [when]
- Evening wind down script: [yours]

Day two (48 to 24 hours)

- Dress rehearsal of the morning only: wake at exam day time, exact breakfast, medication timing, departure sequence: [times]
- Low load day plan, hour by hour, because a vacuum fills itself with forums: [entries]
- Movement: [what, when, familiar not novel]
- Screen curfew: [time]

- Sleep protection: tonight's sleep matters more than tomorrow night's.

Day one (final 24 hours)

- No study. Full stop.
- Evening script: [meal that has worked before, wind down sequence, bag untouched by the door]
- Nightstand: pen and pad for the 3 a.m. audit, ten minutes of writing worries down, lights back off (section 10.3).
- Morning: run the rehearsed sequence to the minute. Arrive early. Deploy the sensory kit. Doorway line: this is the body arriving ready.

Contingency lines (fill in advance)

- If work or family deletes a block: [backup slot]
- If a forum or group chat claims a change: verify against [official source] before any response.
- If sleep fails: one bad final night on a well slept week is survivable. Proceed on the rails.

Appendix F: The Failure Forensics Worksheet

Open this only after 72 hours of first aid (section 12.3). The worksheet's job is to convert a felt verdict back into data, and its output is a routing decision, not a judgment.

Stage one: the raw record. Before interpretation, collect: the score report in full, domain by domain; your time data if the report provides it, or your memory of where time went; what the final third of the exam felt like compared to the first; anything unusual about the day (environment, sleep, medication, admin).

Stage two: the five way sort. Distribute the failure, in rough percentages, across these five causes. Most failures are mixtures; force yourself to weight them.

- Knowledge gap: specific domains scored low and you recognize the material as never mastered. Routes to Chapters 3.0 and 4.0: system volume and technique.
- Timing and format failure: you knew items you never reached, or dense stems consumed the clock. Routes to Chapter 5.0: the attack routine, drilled at fatigue, and the extended time application if not yet made.
- Regulation failure: flooding, blanking, spiraling after a bad section, the last hour lost to a nervous system rather than to ignorance. Routes to Chapters 9.0 and 10.0, and to Chapter 11.0's reset rituals for station formats.
- Environment failure: the room itself taxed you measurably (Kylara's vent, the flicker, the surveillance). Routes to Chapter 9.0's three layers and a rebuilt accommodation file.

- Administrative failure: the adjustment never applied for, the deadline missed, the wrong desk. Routes to Chapters 2.0 and 7.0, with externalization this time.

Stage three: the honesty checks. Was the campaign's system still alive in the final month, or had it quietly died weeks before (if dead, that is the finding, and it routes to Chapter 3.0's architecture, not to more hours)? Did any accommodation you held go unused or arrive untrained (section 5.3)? Is burnout or life load the true first cause, in which case the routing is a structured pause with conditions, dates, and witnesses (section 12.4)?

Stage four: the retake decision. Against the eligibility calendar (section 12.5): earliest permitted date, attempts remaining, authorization expiry. Choose the date by readiness markers you write down now, not by the shame clock. Then rebuild the campaign plan from the routed chapters, and only then rebook.

Appendix G: The Testing Body Quick Reference

Policies change and this table dates faster than any other page in this book. Use it as a map of what to look for, then verify everything against the current official publication of your exam program. Search terms that reliably find the right page: the exam name plus "accommodations," "reasonable adjustments," "special arrangements," or "access arrangements."

Large computer testing vendors (Pearson VUE, PSI, Prometric). Accommodation requests usually run through the exam's owning program, not the vendor, even though the vendor delivers the day. Look for: the program's accommodation page, the vendor's comfort aid list (items permitted without approval), documentation guidelines addressed to evaluators, and the separate scheduling channel for accommodated seats. Expect approval before booking, and expect fewer venues to offer separate rooms.

United States professional boards (nursing, bar, medical, accountancy, trades). The board or a designated agency usually decides; deadlines can fall months before the sitting, with bar examiners the strictest common case. Look for: fixed documentation deadlines tied to application windows, published evaluator guidelines, any reciprocity policy honoring prior accommodations on listed standardized tests, and the appeal or reconsideration procedure. The ADA and the Department of Justice testing guidance sit behind all of it (Chapter 6.0).

United Kingdom regulators and awarding bodies (NMC, GDC, GPhC, professional and trade awarding organizations). The Equality Act's reasonable adjustments duty applies; the NMC's test of competence, for example, publishes a reasonable adjustments process with adjustments declared and evidenced at or before booking. Look for: the adjustments policy document, the evidence standard for specific learning difficulties, deadlines relative to booking rather than to the exam, and the complaints route (Chapter 8.0's ladder, UK rungs).

Online proctored programs. A second rulebook applies on top of the exam's: the proctoring conduct rules (movement, gaze, reading aloud, breaks) and the technical requirements. Movement and vocalization accommodations can be requested for online formats and almost never are (section 9.4). Look for: the proctoring rules document, the system test, and the stated procedure for connection failures.

For every body, the five questions that matter. Who decides. What the documentation standard is, and how recent. When the deadline falls, relative to booking and to the exam. How accommodated seats are scheduled, and where. What the appeal route is, and whether test dates extend pending appeal.

Appendix H: Scripts

Words fail under load, so choose them in advance. Adapt freely; the structure is the point. Every script is one message or one sentence long, because length is where nerve goes to die.

Finding the decision desk (phone or email). "I am registered for [exam] in [window]. Could you confirm who reviews accommodation requests for this exam, this organization or [vendor/board], and point me to the current documentation guideline and deadline?"

Confirming receipt. "Thank you. To confirm: my accommodation application was received on [date] and the stated review period is [X]. I will follow up on [date] if I have not heard."

The polite chase. "My application was received on [date], and the stated review period of [X] has now passed. Could you advise on its status? My booking deadline is [date]."

Asking about deadline extension pending appeal (section 8.3). "I intend to appeal the decision dated [date]. Could you confirm whether my test date or eligibility window can be extended pending the outcome of the appeal, and what the procedure is?"

The needs description opener, for anything the menu lacks (section 7.4). "My assessor's report describes the following functional needs rather than a standard accommodation: [two lines]. Could the test center propose arrangements that would meet these on the day? I am happy to discuss options, and I would like whatever is agreed confirmed in writing."

Comfort aid confirmation. "Your published list permits [items]. Could you confirm in writing that these are acceptable at [center] on [date], so there is no confusion at check in?"

In the room, the seat move (section 9.3). "Excuse me, could I move to a different seat? This one has [noise/light issue] that is affecting my concentration."

In the room, the agreed arrangements. "Good morning. I have written confirmation of agreed arrangements for today, here is the letter, could we take a moment to confirm the desk staff have it too?"

Telling people a result, once, without an autopsy (section 12.3). "I did not pass this attempt. I am taking a few days before I look at the details, and I will figure out next steps after that. I do not need advice yet, but thank you."

The one for yourself, before the door. This is the body arriving ready.

References

ADA Amendments Act of 2008, Pub. L. No. 110-325, 122 Stat. 3553 (2008). https://www.eeoc.gov/statutes/ada-amendments-act-2008

Advokat, C. (2010). What are the cognitive effects of stimulant medications? Emphasis on adults with attention-deficit/hyperactivity disorder (ADHD). *Neuroscience & Biobehavioral Reviews*, *34*(8), 1256-1266. https://doi.org/10.1016/j.neubiorev.2010.03.006

American Psychiatric Association. (2022). *Diagnostic and statistical manual of mental disorders* (5th ed., text rev.). American Psychiatric Publishing.

Americans with Disabilities Act of 1990, 42 U.S.C. § 12101 et seq. (1990). https://www.ada.gov

Ashinoff, B. K., & Abu-Akel, A. (2021). Hyperfocus: The forgotten frontier of attention. *Psychological Research*, *85*(1), 1-19. https://doi.org/10.1007/s00426-019-01245-8

Baddeley, A. (2012). Working memory: Theories, models, and controversies. *Annual Review of Psychology*, *63*, 1-29. https://doi.org/10.1146/annurev-psych-120710-100422

Barkley, R. A. (2015). *Attention-deficit hyperactivity disorder: A handbook for diagnosis and treatment* (4th ed.). Guilford Press.

Beilock, S. (2010). *Choke: What the secrets of the brain reveal about getting it right when you have to*. Free Press.

Beilock, S. L., & Carr, T. H. (2001). On the fragility of skilled performance: What governs choking under pressure? *Journal of Experimental Psychology: General*, *130*(4), 701-725. https://doi.org/10.1037/0096-3445.130.4.701

Bjork, E. L., & Bjork, R. A. (2011). Making things hard on yourself, but in a good way: Creating desirable difficulties to enhance learning. In M. A. Gernsbacher, R. W. Pew, L. M. Hough, & J. R. Pomerantz (Eds.), *Psychology and the real world: Essays illustrating fundamental contributions to society* (pp. 56-64). Worth Publishers.

Brooks, A. W. (2014). Get excited: Reappraising pre-performance anxiety as excitement. *Journal of Experimental Psychology: General*, *143*(3), 1144-1158. https://doi.org/10.1037/a0035325

Brown, T. E. (2013). *A new understanding of ADHD in children and adults: Executive function impairments*. Routledge.

Cage, E., & Troxell-Whitman, Z. (2019). Understanding the reasons, contexts and costs of camouflaging for autistic adults. *Journal of Autism and Developmental Disorders*, *49*(5), 1899-1911. https://doi.org/10.1007/s10803-018-03878-x

Cepeda, N. J., Pashler, H., Vul, E., Wixted, J. T., & Rohrer, D. (2006). Distributed practice in verbal recall tasks: A review and quantitative synthesis. *Psychological Bulletin*, *132*(3), 354-380. https://doi.org/10.1037/0033-2909.132.3.354

Cortese, S., Adamo, N., Del Giovane, C., Mohr-Jensen, C., Hayes, A. J., Carucci, S., Atkinson, L. Z., Tessari, L., Banaschewski, T., Coghill, D., Hollis, C., Simonoff, E., Zuddas, A., Barbui, C., Purgato, M., Steinhausen, H. C., Shokraneh, F., Xia, J., & Cipriani, A. (2018). Comparative efficacy and tolerability of medications for attention-deficit hyperactivity disorder in children, adolescents, and adults: A systematic review and network meta-analysis. *The Lancet Psychiatry*, *5*(9), 727-738. https://doi.org/10.1016/S2215-0366(18)30269-4

Craik, F. I. M., & Lockhart, R. S. (1972). Levels of processing: A framework for memory research. *Journal of Verbal Learning and Verbal Behavior*, *11*(6), 671-684. https://doi.org/10.1016/S0022-5371(72)80001-X

Demetriou, E. A., Lampit, A., Quintana, D. S., Naismith, S. L., Song, Y. J. C., Pye, J. E., Hickie, I., & Guastella, A. J. (2018). Autism spectrum disorders: A meta-analysis of executive function. *Molecular Psychiatry*, *23*(5), 1198-1204. https://doi.org/10.1038/mp.2017.75

Duncan, H., & Purcell, C. (2020). Consensus or contradiction? A review of the current research into the impact of granting extra time in exams to students with specific learning difficulties (SpLD). *Journal of Further and Higher Education*, *44*(4), 439-453. https://doi.org/10.1080/0309877X.2019.1578341

Dunlosky, J., Rawson, K. A., Marsh, E. J., Nathan, M. J., & Willingham, D. T. (2013). Improving students' learning with effective learning techniques: Promising directions from cognitive and educational psychology. *Psychological Science in the Public Interest*, *14*(1), 4-58. https://doi.org/10.1177/1529100612453266

Equality Act 2010, c. 15 (UK). https://www.legislation.gov.uk/ukpga/2010/15/contents

Eysenck, M. W., Derakshan, N., Santos, R., & Calvo, M. G. (2007). Anxiety and cognitive performance: Attentional control theory. *Emotion*, *7*(2), 336-353. https://doi.org/10.1037/1528-3542.7.2.336

Faraone, S. V., Banaschewski, T., Coghill, D., Zheng, Y., Biederman, J., Bellgrove, M. A., Newcorn, J. H., Gignac, M., Al Saud, N. M., Manor, I., Rohde, L. A., Yang, L., Cortese, S., Almagor, D., Stein, M. A., Albatti, T. H., Aljoudi, H. F., Alqahtani, M. M. J., Asherson, P., ... Wang, Y. (2021). The World Federation of ADHD International Consensus Statement: 208 evidence-based conclusions about the disorder. *Neuroscience & Biobehavioral Reviews*, *128*, 789-818. https://doi.org/10.1016/j.neubiorev.2021.01.022

Gathercole, S. E., & Alloway, T. P. (2008). *Working memory and learning: A practical guide for teachers*. SAGE Publications.

Gilbert, P. (2009). *The compassionate mind: A new approach to life's challenges*. Constable & Robinson.

Gordon, M., & Keiser, S. (Eds.). (1998). *Accommodations in higher education under the Americans with Disabilities Act: A no-nonsense guide for clinicians, educators, administrators, and lawyers*. Guilford Press.

Hofmann, S. G., Sawyer, A. T., Witt, A. A., & Oh, D. (2010). The effect of mindfulness-based therapy on anxiety and depression: A meta-analytic review. *Journal of Consulting and Clinical Psychology*, *78*(2), 169-183. https://doi.org/10.1037/a0018555

Hull, L., Petrides, K. V., Allison, C., Smith, P., Baron-Cohen, S., Lai, M. C., & Mandy, W. (2017). "Putting on my best normal": Social camouflaging in adults with autism spectrum conditions. *Journal of Autism and Developmental Disorders*, *47*(8), 2519-2534. https://doi.org/10.1007/s10803-017-3166-5

Hupfeld, K. E., Abagis, T. R., & Shah, P. (2019). Living "in the zone": Hyperfocus in adult ADHD. *ADHD Attention Deficit and Hyperactivity Disorders*, *11*(2), 191-208. https://doi.org/10.1007/s12402-018-0272-y

In the Matter of Antavis Chavis, Misc. No. 65, Sept. Term 2022 (Md. Dec. 21, 2023). https://www.mdcourts.gov/data/opinions/coa/2023/65a22.pdf

Karpicke, J. D., & Blunt, J. R. (2011). Retrieval practice produces more learning than elaborative studying with concept mapping. *Science*, *331*(6018), 772-775. https://doi.org/10.1126/science.1199327

Khan, K. Z., Ramachandran, S., Gaunt, K., & Pushkar, P. (2013). The objective structured clinical examination (OSCE): AMEE Guide No. 81. Part I: An historical and theoretical perspective. *Medical*

Teacher, *35*(9), e1437-e1446. https://doi.org/10.3109/0142159X.2013.818634

Knouse, L. E., & Safren, S. A. (2010). Current status of cognitive behavioral therapy for adult attention-deficit hyperactivity disorder. *Psychiatric Clinics of North America*, *33*(3), 497-509. https://doi.org/10.1016/j.psc.2010.04.001

Kooij, J. J. S., Bijlenga, D., Salerno, L., Jaeschke, R., Bitter, I., Balázs, J., Thome, J., Dom, G., Kasper, S., Nunes Filipe, C., Stes, S., Mohr, P., Leppämäki, S., Casas, M., Bobes, J., McCarthy, J. M., Richarte, V., Kjems Philipsen, A., Pehlivanidis, A., ... Asherson, P. (2019). Updated European Consensus Statement on diagnosis and treatment of adult ADHD. *European Psychiatry*, *56*, 14-34. https://doi.org/10.1016/j.eurpsy.2018.11.001

Lim, J., & Dinges, D. F. (2010). A meta-analysis of the impact of short-term sleep deprivation on cognitive variables. *Psychological Bulletin*, *136*(3), 375-389. https://doi.org/10.1037/a0018883

Lovett, B. J. (2010). Extended time testing accommodations for students with disabilities: Answers to five fundamental questions. *Review of Educational Research*, *80*(4), 611-638. https://doi.org/10.3102/0034654310364063

Lovett, B. J., & Lewandowski, L. J. (2015). *Testing accommodations for students with disabilities: Research-based practice*. American Psychological Association.

MacLennan, K., O'Brien, S., & Tavassoli, T. (2022). In our own words: The complex sensory experiences of autistic adults. *Journal of Autism and Developmental Disorders*, *52*(7), 3061-3075. https://doi.org/10.1007/s10803-021-05186-3

Milton, D. E. M. (2012). On the ontological status of autism: The 'double empathy problem'. *Disability & Society*, *27*(6), 883-887. https://doi.org/10.1080/09687599.2012.710008

Murray, D., Lesser, M., & Lawson, W. (2005). Attention, monotropism and the diagnostic criteria for autism. *Autism*, *9*(2), 139-156. https://doi.org/10.1177/1362361305051398

National Conference of Bar Examiners. (2016). Reviewing ADHD accommodations requests for the bar exam: What has and has not changed over 20 years. *The Bar Examiner*, *85*(2). https://thebarexaminer.ncbex.org

Neff, K. D. (2003). Self-compassion: An alternative conceptualization of a healthy attitude toward oneself. *Self and Identity*, *2*(2), 85-101. https://doi.org/10.1080/15298860309032

Nelson, J. M., & Harwood, H. (2011). Learning disabilities and anxiety: A meta-analysis. *Journal of Learning Disabilities*, *44*(1), 3-17. https://doi.org/10.1177/0022219409359939

Nursing and Midwifery Council. (2021). *Test of competence 2021: OSCE information booklet for nurses*. Nursing and Midwifery Council. https://www.nmc.org.uk

Prevatt, F., & Levrini, A. (2015). *ADHD coaching: A guide for mental health professionals*. American Psychological Association.

Putnam, A. L., Sungkhasettee, V. W., & Roediger, H. L. (2016). Optimizing learning in college: Tips from cognitive psychology. *Perspectives on Psychological Science*, *11*(5), 652-660. https://doi.org/10.1177/1745691616645770

Ramirez, G., & Beilock, S. L. (2011). Writing about testing worries boosts exam performance in the classroom. *Science*, *331*(6014), 211-213. https://doi.org/10.1126/science.1199427

Ramsay, J. R., & Rostain, A. L. (2015). *Cognitive-behavioral therapy for adult ADHD: An integrative psychosocial and medical approach* (2nd ed.). Routledge.

Raymaker, D. M., Teo, A. R., Steckler, N. A., Lentz, B., Scharer, M., Delos Santos, A., Kapp, S. K., Hunter, M., Joyce, A., & Nicolaidis, C. (2020). "Having all of your internal resources exhausted beyond measure and being left with no clean-up crew": Defining autistic burnout. *Autism in Adulthood*, *2*(2), 132-143. https://doi.org/10.1089/aut.2019.0079

Rayner, K., Schotter, E. R., Masson, M. E. J., Potter, M. C., & Treiman, R. (2016). So much to read, so little time: How do we read, and can speed reading help? *Psychological Science in the Public Interest*, *17*(1), 4-34. https://doi.org/10.1177/1529100615623267

Rehabilitation Act of 1973, 29 U.S.C. § 701 et seq. (1973).

Robertson, A. E., & Simmons, D. R. (2013). The relationship between sensory sensitivity and autistic traits in the general population. *Journal of Autism and Developmental Disorders*, *43*(4), 775-784. https://doi.org/10.1007/s10803-012-1608-7

Roediger, H. L., & Karpicke, J. D. (2006). Test-enhanced learning: Taking memory tests improves long-term retention. *Psychological Science*, *17*(3), 249-255. https://doi.org/10.1111/j.1467-9280.2006.01693.x

Safren, S. A., Otto, M. W., Sprich, S., Winett, C. L., Wilens, T. E., & Biederman, J. (2005). Cognitive-behavioral therapy for ADHD in medication-treated adults with continued symptoms. *Behaviour Research and Therapy*, *43*(7), 831-842. https://doi.org/10.1016/j.brat.2004.07.001

Sedgwick, J. A., Merwood, A., & Asherson, P. (2019). The positive aspects of attention deficit hyperactivity disorder: A qualitative investigation of successful adults with ADHD. *ADHD Attention Deficit and Hyperactivity Disorders*, *11*(3), 241-253. https://doi.org/10.1007/s12402-018-0277-6

Shaw, P., Stringaris, A., Nigg, J., & Leibenluft, E. (2014). Emotion dysregulation in attention deficit hyperactivity disorder. *American Journal of Psychiatry*, *171*(3), 276-293. https://doi.org/10.1176/appi.ajp.2013.13070966

Sireci, S. G., Scarpati, S. E., & Li, S. (2005). Test accommodations for students with disabilities: An analysis of the interaction hypothesis. *Review of Educational Research*, *75*(4), 457-490. https://doi.org/10.3102/00346543075004457

Sirois, F., & Pychyl, T. (2013). Procrastination and the priority of short-term mood regulation: Consequences for future self. *Social and Personality Psychology Compass*, *7*(2), 115-127. https://doi.org/10.1111/spc3.12011

Snowling, M. J., Hulme, C., & Nation, K. (2020). Defining and understanding dyslexia: Past, present and future. *Oxford Review of Education*, *46*(4), 501-513. https://doi.org/10.1080/03054985.2020.1765756

Solanto, M. V. (2011). *Cognitive-behavioral therapy for adult ADHD: Targeting executive dysfunction*. Guilford Press.

Steel, P. (2007). The nature of procrastination: A meta-analytic and theoretical review of quintessential self-regulatory failure. *Psychological Bulletin*, *133*(1), 65-94. https://doi.org/10.1037/0033-2909.133.1.65

Swanson, H. L., & Hsieh, C. J. (2009). Reading disabilities in adults: A selective meta-analysis of the literature. *Review of Educational Research*, *79*(4), 1362-1390. https://doi.org/10.3102/0034654309350931

U.S. Department of Justice, Civil Rights Division. (2014). *ADA requirements: Testing accommodations*. U.S. Department of Justice. https://www.ada.gov/resources/testing-accommodations/

von der Embse, N., Jester, D., Roy, D., & Post, J. (2018). Test anxiety effects, predictors, and correlates: A 30-year meta-analytic review. *Journal of Affective Disorders*, *227*, 483-493. https://doi.org/10.1016/j.jad.2017.11.048

Walker, M. (2017). *Why we sleep: Unlocking the power of sleep and dreams*. Scribner.

Zeidner, M. (1998). *Test anxiety: The state of the art*. Plenum Press.

www.ingramcontent.com/pod-product-compliance
Lightning Source LLC
LaVergne TN
LVHW022108200926
848481LV00003B/1110
* 9 7 9 8 9 0 5 9 9 3 0 0 8 *